The Pen Perrir

Stories of Northwest Orange County Florida

Perrine Slim

Writings from

3 April 2009
to
16 December 2011

Publication Date 2015 January
Olmstead Publishing LLC

The Pennings of Perrine Slim:
Stories of Northwest Orange County Florida
ISBN 978-1-934194-27-0 paper

Perrine Slim, Author
Francina Boykin, Assisted
Phyllis M. Olmstead, Editor, Cover Artist, marked photographs
Annie Belle Gilliam, Copywriter, Museum Curator
Angela Nicols, Planner
Christine Hammett, Graphic Technician

Text similarly published in *The Apopka Chief*
Photos marked AHS are of the Apopka Historical Society

Olmstead Publishing LLC
olmsteadpublishing@usa.com

A project for the Apopka Historical Society
Museum of the Apopkans
122 E Fifth St
Apopka, Florida 32703
(407) 703-1707
www.Facebook.com/MuseumoftheApopkans
www.ApopkaMuseum.org

www.facebook.com/olmsteadpublishing
www.OlmsteadPublishing.com
www.SquareUp.com/Market/Olmstead-Publishing-LLC

This book is dedicated to the hardworking and long suffering people of color who dared to venture into the mosquito, snake, and alligator filled area of Central Florida in the area to become Northwest Orange County in the vicinity of Ahapopka, now called Apopka.

Table of Contents

Stories of Northwest Orange County Florida

List of Images

Noun Usage: As time progresses, words take on different meanings and events in history make words more intense or even lose their original purpose. Perrine Slim uses many words interchangeably as they were used during different decades of his life to mean the same thing.

The author prefers the term "below the TO&A tracks" to the term "South Apopka". He lovingly and humorously uses the colloquialisms ghetto, projects, Soulsville, blackbelt, hood, and slums to mean the area below the the TO&A tracks. He refers to people of his "ethnicity" as Negroes, coloreds, colored people, blacks, soulmen, soul sisters, soul brothers, and people of color in different articles in this tome.

Years—Understanding the Terminology

- A century is 100 years. The 19th century includes the dates January 1, 1801–December 31, 1900.
- A decade is 10 years. 1801-1810 is a decade.
- The third decade of the 20th century is 1921-1930.
- The 1960s are the years 1960-1969.

The Apopka Chief, April 3, 2009, Page 14A

Politicians influenced local citrus industry

Early 20th Century Apopka Politicians and the Citrus Era

William Brown "W. B." Goding's influence on politics and citrus production:

Slim recalls from history records that The Lodge area was the focal point of interest and living accommodations in the 1850s-1875. Individuals and families yearned to move from the central location of the city, as it was known then, into nearby villages, namely Merrimack, Rock Springs, and Bay Ridge. Even today, the heretofore-mentioned areas are considered prime areas for establishing roots for many families.

Alfred and Sarah Goding moved from Georgia around 1890 into Bay Ridge, meeting numerous individuals that started growth and enterprises in the area, namely F. M. Trobridge, Adam Stewart, Henry Schopke, H. D. Hood, and W. C. Brooks.

Alfred Goding became extremely interested in citrus caretaking and hunting preservation immediately after the disastrous freezes of 1894-1895, when many citrus growers, due to the economic crisis in that era along with Mother Nature's severe abnormal weather conditions. This suddenly caused the average citrus grower to cease citrus farming. Goding remained in the area and gained credibility in agriculture and hunting preserve ventures. In approximately 1930, W. B. Goding was president of the famous Apopka Sportsmen's Club that had acquired [less than 6,000] acres of prime hunting preserve between Rock Springs and Wekiwa Springs.

In 1931, Richard Whitney purchased the Florida Insecticide Company and made W. B. Goding general manager. Approximately five years later, it merged with Stauffer Chemical Company of Texas. During World War II, the plant used German war prisoners as workers to manufacture certain insecticides or fertilizers. In the early 1950s, the plant completely moved its operations to Tampa. W. B. Goding, due to his expertise in citrus caretaking and the availability of products from Stauffer Chemical Company, teamed up with Arlie Franklin Gilliam, one of the area's outstanding citrus grove caretakers, naming their business Goding & Gilliam Grove Service. Slim, being an advocate of citrus growing, cultivation and chemical application was fortunate to have known both men personally for their scientific information pertaining to citrus caretaking. Slim on occasion would make purchases at Stauffer Chemical and frequent one of their grove service barns in Apopka at the corner of Fifth Street and South Park Avenue during the 1940s.

1 The State Bank of Apopka board @ 1948. Top-Frank Burgust, Thomas Swanner. Sitting-Jack Camp, Edwin Fly, Robert Carlton, Henry Land. Photo Apopka Historical Society (AHS)

In 1934, after the demise of William Edwards, then the president of the State Bank of Apopka, Goding, along with the likes of W. T. Champneys, R. T. Carlton and Richard Whitney, were elected to the bank's board. In 1935, he was elected as an Apopka city commissioner, along with newly elected Gillen McClure as mayor. Goding's tenure as commissioner was very influential on numerous issues pertaining to delinquent taxes, entrepreneurships, local and township borders as to where people of different ethnic backgrounds would live.

In July 1937, the City of Apopka council enacted an ordinance designating segregated areas as to where whites or blacks could live or promote businesses. Specifically for Negroes, this area was below the Tavares, Orlando & Atlantic Railroad (TO&A Railroad) tracks and east of the Midland Railroad tracks.

2 The Tracks. To the right, black people could not live or congregate. To the left was "the other side of the tracks". Jim Crow segregation July 1937. Photo DrO 2014 12 29

Another issue that was a prevalent problem with the city had to do with delinquent property tax issues that were used in forcing blacks to move from above the railroad tracks. This aided in the constant efforts to enforce the Jim Crow system by any means that the powers to be considered politically correct. Nevertheless, Morris Chisholm, Sr., a Negro, along with an influential neighbor, fought vigorously to overturn that ordinance.

Initially, the ordinance contained zero tolerance as to where Negroes could live and where they congregated for work transportation. After numerous complaints from a few white citizens, companies employing blacks that needed transportation to work, told the workers they should congregate only below the TO&A Railroad tracks to be picked up for work transportation. One of these many companies, Apopka's Hamrick & Hamrick Lumber Company and Consumers Lumber & Veneer Company constructed housing (quarters) accommodations on their mill sites for colored employees in order to avoid being in conflict with the ordinance. The ordinance was eventually repealed in March 1968.

Many years after the 1968 repeal, workers requiring transportation staged their activity at South Central Avenue and Ninth Street well into the

20th century. Nowadays, since temporary job service companies provide services, they have numerous office facilities and staging areas above the railroad tracks where workers congregate before being assigned.

> **Jim Crow Laws existed in Apopka, Florida from July 1937 - March 1968**

The law that was discussed in the previous paragraph certainly would have had full support of councilperson W. B. Goding in the 1930s. He originally sought a means of restricting the movements of non-whites in the community after complaints from white citizens.

Citrus production and caretaking in the 1940s, as Slim recalls, was one of the chief industries for the average local family's livelihood, and William Brown "W. B. Goding and his renowned citrus caretaking partner, Arlie Gilliam, were number one in their fields of endeavor. These gentlemen were a pair with whom Slim conversed on numerous occasions.

Slim thanks W. B. Goding and his immediate family for the insight relative to citrus they so willingly gave to the area.

3 Garrett Gilliam, Jr. with grove managers Garrett Gilliam and William Brown Goding in Arlie Gilliam's grove, father of Garrett. Photo from Gilliam family.

Tavares, Orlando & Atlantic Railroad Company (TO&A) incorporated in 1883.
Sold to Florida Railway and Navigation Company, resold to Florida Central & Peninsular Railroad Company in 1891.
Sold to Seaboard Air Line Railway (SAL) in 1903.
Author uses TO&A and SAL interchangably.

The Apopka Chief, April 17, 2009, Page 11A

School bus stop part of South Apopka history

Ninth and Tenth Streets at Central Avenue

Since the late 1920s, the area mentioned in the title has been a focal point of interest for Negroes in Apopka pertaining to academia and public gatherings.

Opportunities for educational achievement for Negroes in the 19th century in the Apopka community began with St. Paul AME Church, which had the gigantic task of establishing academic facilities to accommodate pupils for academic programs at Johnson Town, Sarah Mead's Bottom, and South Robinson Avenue until the State of Florida, along with Orange County, assumed total responsibility for maintaining and building academic curriculum and administrative staff for teaching.

4 Cornerstone of St Paul AME Church currently at 11th St and Clarcona Rd. Photo Dr. O. 2014 12 29

Once state and county governmental agencies assumed complete stewardship of education in Apopka for the ethnic group previously mentioned, approximately in the 1920s, property was obtained at South Central Avenue between West Ninth and 10th streets, and as recorded, a small amount of the proceeds from a bond issue in 1924 was utilized to upgrade a building in disrepair by adding a new room. However that scanty amount of bond-issue proceeds allotted wasn't quite enough, so the community's Negro citizens to raise monies wherein to continue classroom additions accommodations for the school term an extra month.

Although in 1927, Apopka Colored School (now Phyllis Wheatley) was moved to its present day site at West 18th Street near South Lake Avenue, there tends be a constant gathering of students at Ninth and Tenth streets on Central Avenue on a daily school-day basis, enroute to schools in the area by Orange County Public School bus transportation. Slim recalls, during his tenure as a student (1946) enrolled at Hungerford High School in Eatonville, approximately 80 pupils assembled at S. Central and Ninth Street in order to catch the school bus.

Even today, this means of school bus transportation is very prevalent, but entails different schools. However, it has created many concerns with numerous citizens regarding the student's behavior while they wait for the school bus. Students have no regards or respect for New Hope Missionary Baptist Church's property and Michael Gladden's monument site and that has many concerned citizens hoping that pupils understand the significance of discernment along with behavior.

In conclusion, many citizens are very disgruntled as to the disrespect that students exhibit daily towards two individuals' contributions that are a legacy to the community and their

5 Michael Gladden, Jr. Monument.
Photo Dr.O. 2014 12 29

Negro ethnicity. Mr. George Oden, a renowned pioneer farmer and a devoted member of NHMBC, donated property for the church's site, and Mr. Michael Gladden, an entrepreneur and prominent trusted leader in the community from 1924-1982.

His monument was dedicated by City of Apopka in 1982 and speaks for the mentoring, social, and financial contributions he gave so willingly to his fellowman of this community without reservations. Slim was indeed fortunate to have known both of these outstanding pioneers, personally for a total of 40 years, with a great deal of sincere admiration and absolute respect.

Ms. Mildred A. Board, creator of the Bits 'n' Tips column in *The Apopka Chief* weekly newspaper, would certainly detest the students' behavior patterns, especially when they have been counseled and taught to have respect for their elders, appreciation for their heritage, and last but not least, respect all ethnicity. Ms. Board, in the majority of her writing, constantly insisted students visit the Museum of the Apopkans to ascertain concrete knowledge as to how this town was created with different ethnic groups and their contributions.

6 Teaching a third generation to respect the past. Willie Scott, Newton Bell, Dora Bell Norman, Monica Zow, Phyllis 'Dr. O.' Olmstead, Lenwood Patterson, III, Camari Dennison. Photo by Marlon M. Britten 2014.

The Apopka Chief, April 24, 2009, Page 13A

Basketball became favorite sport in South Apopka

Round Ball History in the Apopka Ghetto

This article pertains to the late Birthel Simpkins Jr., favorably called "Daddy Birt," who was born in the Florida panhandle town Monticello during the 1920s, but nurtured in Polk County and Orange County. The article is mainly in reference to his expertise and efforts he so willingly gave to teach several sports, including the game of basketball, in the Apopka "hood" area. Shortly after completing high school during WWII, he was drafted and served his country honorably for a few years.

Orange County and Apopka were indeed fortunate to have Birthel Jr. living in the area due to the fact his father Birthel Sr. ventured into Apopka after being hired in the 1930s by lumber tycoon Wilson Hamrick of Hamrick & Hamrick Lumber Company of Apopka.

Birthel attended high school in Lakeland around the 1940s, where he became familiar with and mastered many sports games, including basketball. During that era, black kids in Slim's area did not even know about the game. However, with his dedication and instructions during that period, the game of roundball became the pastime sport in the community, with the average home having a basketball goal in or about their premises.

When Birthel Jr., began teaching the game in the 1940s, there were no basketball courts available in the area. Through innovation, utilizing portions of the hard clay road surface of South Central Avenue and 18th Street and after erecting a goal post, backboard, and goal enabled kids to play half-court basketball on the roadway.

Eventually, the Apopka Colored School (also known as Phyllis Wheatley School) gave Daddy Birt permission to establish a full-court on its campus. However, Birthel Jr., had to, on his own time and finances, start a networking arrangement to get several individuals who owned trucks or had access to them to haul clay material to the location, because the Orange County School Board would not be financially responsible for constructing the court.

At this point in time, no ethnic school within Orange County located in the so-called ghettos had the use of a gymnasium; therefore, basketball and similar activities were played in the elements (outdoors). Eventually, Birthel Jr., constructed a fence wall around the perimeter to enclose the court with slab materials obtained through the courtesy of Hamrick & Hamrick. The mill occasionally hauled them to the PWS site, and construction companies donated sheet metal roofing and slabs to be used for fence walls.

Numerous individuals benefited from Birthel Jr.'s efforts, concerns, and instructions relative to sports during his tenure within the neighborhood and his finances and community contributions to construct the basketball court at Apopka Colored School

Residents such as Lee Neil Jr., Quilley Freeman, Louis Garvin, Joseph R. Gladden, Marian White, K. D. Dinkins, Malachi Woods, Fellow Moss, Rossie Thomas Bellamy, Herman "Doc" McQueen, Mary Johnson, Leroy Fillmore, Goose Thomas, Johnny L. Stokes, Freddie Fillmore and many more gained a status of notoriety through his teaching.

7 Each entrance to the area of unicorporated Orange County below Tenth Street, referred to as South Apopka, is proudly marked. Photo Dr.O. 2014 12 29

The Apopka Chief, May 1, 2009, Page 10A

'Old Man' Frank Sharp Sr. had vast citrus acreage

"Old Man" Frank Sharp Sr. of Orlando Orange, Lake and Martin counties citrus grower

Mr. Frank Sharp Sr. was an entrepreneur and prominent citrus grower in several Florida counties, including Lake, Martin, and Orange. His business ventures initiated during the 1930s, when the majority of property that he planted upon was virgin land.

Frank Sharp Sr. definitely had roots, especially in the immediate Orange County area, employing 10-15 persons from Apopka on a daily basis for grove service caretaking well into 1989. His sister married former Orange County Commissioner John Talton of Apopka.

"Old-man Frank Sharp" would often tell Slim of trials and failures he and his early prominent citrus grower neighbors (Dr. Phillips, Roper Bros., Story, Bradshaw, Chase, R. D. Keene, McKinnon, Connelly, Fowler, Tilden, and several other prominent growers not intentionally omitted) encountered during those infant years of citrus production. His vast acreage of citrus groves in the 1930s–1950s was in the Reedy Creek district of southwest

Orange County (adjacent to the area that is the present day Walt Disney World properties, and some also belonged to Apopka's lumber tycoons Wilson and Carroll Hamrick of Hamrick & Hamrick Lumber Company owned).

He and his brother, , negotiated and purchased 648 acres of property that was blessed with several fresh water lakes (Lake Sharp, Lake Reams, and Lake Spar) of sizeable acreage located at CR 535 and Reams Road in 1934. This vast section has a beautiful home constructed from the pine and oak timbers harvested at that point in time on the heretofore-mentioned potential grove land. This home is still intact and maintained with tender loving care as of this penning. An area he called the Bay Head grove area, which had tremendous acreage of timbers (primarily both species of the cone-bearing evergreen trees of the pine tree family—cypress and needle-leafed pines) south of Reams Road, was acquired by Walt Disney in the 1970s, and utilized as mobile home living quarters for their employees.

Often, Sharp would tell Slim it cost more to clear the virgin properties than what they paid for it. As for the land clearing in the 1930s-1940s, it was accomplished by hand grubbing, mules and machines they purchased from Pounds Motor

Company of Winter Garden over a period of time. Orlando's newspaper publisher, editor, and owner, Martin Andersen from Mississippi, sold the brothers an established bearing citrus grove of mixed varieties (Hamlin, Valencia, Murcott). The approximately 400 acres, called the "Sentinel Star Grove," was located in the Reedy Creek district south of Seidel Road and west of CR 545, where Reedy Creek crosses beneath CR 545, discharging into the swampy area next to the existing grove purchased from Orlando's newspaper publisher Martin Andersen.

The Reams Road grove area, at one point in time, was an important portion of the swamp distilling area that Orange County agricultural agent Henry Swanson, following years of extensive research studies, referred to as the cleansing house for waters that flowed from East Orange County to the southwest of Orange County. Numerous ditches and underground culvert piping were amassed throughout the Reams Road grove, especially during the 1960s-1970s, to drain water from the rows of citrus trees and distribute excess waters to retention ponds, the main swamp and areas adjacent to the grove perimeters.

These retention ponds were extremely significant whenever irrigating or using water for herbicide or applying citrus spray materials. This eliminated excessive time and distance traveled in order to obtain water for these designated grove areas. A similar situation at the 65-acre Mascotte grove, located at Simon Brown Road and SR 33 in Mascotte, had ditches and water holding ponds that were employed to receive excessive water to alleviate water-logged tree rows.

The Mascotte grove had a variety of fruit, including Hamlins as the prominent fruit plus a five-acre addition of Orlando Tangelos that separated the east section from west section of the grove. Although the majority of the groves had an abundance of surface water, there was usually difficulty within tree rows. The dry seasons precipitated installing complete underground piping irrigation system to supply overhead sprinklers, and giant gun impact traveling sprinklers. The groves in Orlando around the Conway Lakes area were basically the older groves and the Conway Lakes chain was very significant in supplying waters for numerous operations pertaining to citrus maintenance.

One grove, in particular, near Gatlin Road in Orlando that was not too far from the U.S. Navy Underwater Research Center, received much interest for being near Little Lake Conway. Progress in the arena of urbanizing has terminated the majority of Mr. Sharp's citrus holdings in the Orlando area. Believe it or not, at this point and time, in certain areas of Orange County, citrus trees can only be seen in a museum (smile). Mother nature taught "Old Man Sharp" where to plant citrus trees that he and his sons (John Sr., and Frank Jr.) passed down to Slim's tenure, after numerous attempts at challenging the abnormal weather and soil conditions in order for them to survive and be productive.

8 Garrett Gilliam (l), unknown citrus harvester (c), W. B. Goding (r).
photo from AHS

In many cases, you could observe several acres in which no trees were planted and that was because it was, environmentally, in the best interest not to plant. Mr. Frank Sharp, was indeed a conscientious, caring, concerned grovesman and totally believed in God as an individual. Slim often shared God's given spiritual beliefs with Mr. Sharp.

In conclusion, Slim thanks "Old Man Sharp" his wife, their children, John Sr., Fran, Rita and Frank Jr., for allowing Slim to serve as superintendent of Sharp's Groves, Inc (initiating in approximately 1970 and climaxing January 1, 1990). The December 1989 disastrous freeze totally eliminated the groves and Slim's tenure; however, Slim keeps in touch especially around any political election, mainly because the family was much involved in politics and willing shared their experiences without blemish.

The Apopka Chief, May 8, 2009, Page 12A

Muck farms were a big part of Apopka's history

Migrant Workers of the 1940s-1980s

Most persons nurtured in the "hood," "blackbelt," or "ghetto" have experienced at least one phase of farming due to the fact it was a ways and means at that point in time for the entire family's survival in this area, beginning as early as the mid-1940s and going well into the 1990s.

In the early 20th century, in approximately 1904, James "Sawgrass" Jones, who was nurtured in Tennessee, ventured into Zellwood from Texas. He has to be written about, because he played a very significant role in establishing and recruiting families in the area for muckland farming, due to the advancement at that time of machine technology, lake water level control and scientific agriculture studies.

Lake Apopka's mucklands, even during the Seminole Indian era, served as a catalyst for food and financial gains for Indians, as well as white settlers and Negroes. Sawgrass Jones' primary interest involved how quickly the soil and weather conditions would enhance the growth of agriculture products that he was not accustomed to in the states in which he was nurtured, but were much in demand due to the products' nutritional capabilities.

9 Timucuan canoe fragment discovered in muckland on Charlie Grinnell's muck farm near Plymouth. Estimated construction 1,200-1,500 A.D. . See in the Museum of the Apopkans, 122 E 5th St. Photo by DrO 2014.

At a speaking engagement in October 2008 at the United Methodist Church of Zellwood, Slim had the most memorable privilege to meet Charlie Grinnell, such an "antique aged" individual and discuss some of the old timers like Sawgrass Jones, Edwin Fly, William Edwards, and Richard Whitney, most of whom Mr. Grinnell knew personally due to their involvement in the mucklands. Charlie is almost 100 years old and had come to Zellwood as a very, very young adult, curious as to what the mucklands offered.

Slim recalls, as a boy in the 1940s, muckland farming became extremely prevalent on Lake Apopka at that point in time, with the new numerous pioneer farmers (of that era), whose interest and endeavors of the muckland farming benefited the areas enormously. The Hoopers, A. Duda & Sons, Longs, Letsingers, Lusts, Franks,

Stroups, Crumps, Beech-Nut Foods, Scotts, Zellwin Farms and several other farmers specialized in greens, potatoes, sugarcane, string beans, kale, parsley, squash, cucumbers, peppers, and chicory.

All personnel were needed for cultivation while plants matured waiting harvesting. Several individuals of Negro ethnicity, namely Linda Lee, Henry Ellison, Viola Robinson, Clara Neal, Margie Lee, Elizabeth R. Garner, Carrie Belle R. Cunningham, Mann Riggins, Alfred Robinson, and Jeremiah Neal managed hand crews for these farmers.

These crews consisted of women who were paid by the hour or on a daily basis for service rendered pertaining to airing, pruning, fertilizing, pest control application, or weeding during the entire cultivation period for the above mentioned muckland farmers. Once the cultivation periods climaxed, most workers went into harvesting and most firms paid wages by piece production. It was necessary that the crew leaders, at that time of cultivation and harvesting, owned a flat-bedded truck with full-length benches on both sides and one full-length bench in the center with a tent-like cover that allowed sitting, standing, and protection from the elements to transport workers back and forth wherever needed.

Sweet corn, normally produced extensively in the midwest United States, made its debut on the Florida mucklands after thorough research studies in 1940s-1950s regarding disease resistance, maturity period, quality, cultivation involvement, marketing and financial gains.

However, its prominence appeared full throttle in 1969, bringing an overwhelming stability to areas such as employment, marketing and economy. During the heretofore-mentioned era well into the 1980s, sweet corn production, along with other minor vegetables, were a key booster for the area's growth and economic stability. Scientists, after many years of concrete research analysis, found ample traces of nitrates and other sources of chemicals that contaminated Lake Apopka, precipitated from chemical run-offs utilized for muckland farming. This created an unbalanced ecological system, which would cause Lake Apopka's demise if not corrected immediately. Farmers of the mucklands, along with the state of Florida, have consolidated means and efforts as a future preventive measure.

10 Students from Rollins College ethics course listen to Office For Farmworker Ministry discuss the farmworkers depicted on the memorial quilt and the consequences of DDT and other chemical exposures over the decades. Photo Dr.O. 2013 02 01

Builder puts expertise to good use

Building Contractor in Low Socio-Economic Areas--HIP Homes

Lamar Hughley is a renowned builder whose expertise lays in concrete cinder blocks, foundations (footers), floors, and driveways. Lamar has pursued this form of specific endeavor for more than twenty years in Osceola, Sumter, Lake, Seminole, and Orange counties.

Hughley was nurtured in Florida for most of his adolescent span of life, along with seven siblings. He attended Phyllis Wheatley Elementary School and Apopka Memorial High School in Apopka to obtain the necessary academic requirements for graduation at both schools. He attended Lane College in Jackson, Tennessee, as a freshman, where he excelled as a football player during his tenure.

During the summer months into mid-October every year, his father, Charlie Hughley Sr., an apple orchard caretaker, ventured into Pennsylvania and New York, taking the entire family for endeavors pertaining to apples.

Lamar, at that point in time, after completing high school and enrolling in college, was very conscientious regarding the heretofore-mentioned endeavors relative to concrete products. During this period, he met Martineau Ivey Sr., an established cinder block mason, who was several years ahead of Lamar's actual experiences in that type of work and was well renowned and respected for his craftsmanship, even in today's market, within the building trades arena. Eventually, they (Ivey and Hughley) created a partnership that allowed Lamar to obtain immeasurable knowledge in the concrete trade. It lasted for several years until protocols previously negotiated by the two parties could not be resolved. This situation forced the two parties to relinquish the partnership. With the knowledge Lamar Hughley gained from the partnership, he established a legitimate company of his own, where he could be insured and licensed by the state and federal governments in order to receive bona fide contracts for jobs offered.

Currently, the majority of contracts Lamar receive stems from Homes In Partnership, a developer of homes to accommodate low-income families in the Central Florida area. This work enables him to employ approximately eight qualified individuals five days per week.

Lamar has keen interest in civic affairs that enhance neighborhood relations for self-esteem. One of his primary projects is relative to the development of teenagers, academically and socially, to develop their sense of responsibility. The interest in teenagers was precipitated by the tragic demise of his son (Lamar Hughley Jr.) in 2006 in an accident involving a four-wheeler ATV in Apopka. His grieving for his son interrupted his business interest briefly.

However, with persistence and consolation from his immediate family, especially his biological sister, Lynn Kara Hughley, to alleviate his constant grief, they conceived the idea of motivating teenagers to cope with life's responsibilities, along with divine spiritual involvement. This encouraged Lamar to purchase a facility on South Central Avenue near Tenth Street in Apopka, which was previously the Ace Colored Theatre, to establish a youth center in his son's honor for purposes of meetings, recreation, learning, and certain vocational skills which he would constantly oversee, along with family members. At this time, due to specific building code statutes, the project has been temporarily placed on hold.

11 1941 Ace Colored Theatre playbill. Located in the Museum of the Apopkans.

The Orange County Sheriff's Office initiated a community policing organization, whose interest was establishing a Neighborhood Watch program. Lamarwas designated for recruiting membership for the area below the Tavares, Orlando & Atlantic (TO&A) railroad tracks in Apopka.

Lamar also headed up the Men's Club in Apopka, which has been well received within the community for having assisted the needy whenever called upon. This organization has done this for numerous years and still maintains its purposes.

Slim, along with many other citizens in the area, want to thank Lamar Hughley personally, as well as his dedicated family for their kindness, compassion, concern and materialistic input they have done for the community.

The Apopka Chief, June 12, 2009, Page 13A

Apopka woman taught at same school she attended

A Schoolmarm to be Remembered--A Competent, Renowned OCPS Teacher

This is one of Slim's articles that he enjoys the most because it is relative to the desire and performance of people in areas pertaining to their educational achievements and to individuals who have devoted tremendous amounts of time, concern, compassion, material attributes, and dedication to the teaching profession.

Bobbie Lois Green McKenzie, an Apopka-bred person, was brought up below the TO&A Railroad tracks on Ninth Street (Michael Gladden Blvd.) while attending Phyllis Wheatley Elementary and Phyllis Wheatley High School, graduating shortly after the 20th century halfway mark. Ms. Bobbie Lois, as so favorably called by all, regardless of age, ethnicity or public status, first attended college in Marion County for a short stint before relocating to Bethune-Cookman College (now known as Bethune-Cookman University) in Daytona Beach, where she obtained a degree in education.

Upon graduation, she signed a contract with Orange County Public Schools for Phyllis Wheatley Elementary School, where she remained as a competent, renowned classroom teacher among her peers, students and OCPS administers for approximately 40 years. She gives credit to Jehovah God, her mother, Mrs. Ethel M. Green, and PWES' principal at that point in time, Mrs. Marie S. Gladden, who was considered an elite administrator throughout Orange and Seminole counties.

Often Ms. Bobbie Lois would tell Slim about numerous encounters she had with Mrs. Gladden that were extremely beneficial in her decisions regarding teaching methods – things such as Friday's dress-down day, pupil behavior, lesson plans for the week and, by all means, teacher's decisions relative to discernment on educational and way-of-life instructions.

She and her husband, Clifford McKenzie, are still, nowadays, devoted practicing Christians at New Hope Missionary Baptist Church in Apopka, and have been since their childhood days. They have two adult daughters employed in the academic system in the state of Florida.

Slim, as usual, has always considered it a privilege and honor to recall educational attributes and methods of teaching with this illustrious individual, who has contributed an enormous amount of effort and skill pertaining to education.

Ms. Bobbie Lois, Slim has to comment that, due to the fact that he's truly a senior citizen beyond your years, he and two other neighborhood kids (Mary Jane Howard and Moses Howard Jr.) would baby-sit with you with milk bottles and diapers for a few hours while your mother Mrs. Ethel, the proprietor, supervised the Green's Dry Cleaning and Pressing business (smile).

Believe me, your teaching skills and what they meant still impress many past and present citizens in the ghetto, projects, Soulsville, blackbelt area below the TO&A railroad tracks. Thank you, Ms. Bobbie Lois, thank you. Even nowadays, Slim has been informed that you, along with several other retired educators, allot time and efforts towards upgrading many current pupils' gray matter. The impact of concerns, relationships, and improvements within our communities with retirees' involvement has indeed made a difference beyond reproach.

12 Apopka Chief of Police Joseph C. Brown, Jr. June 8, 1995-
March 16, 2004. Photo AHS.

13 Apopka Chief of Police Tom Collins, January 11, 1971-
November 21, 1990. Photo AHS.

The Apopka Chief, June 26, 2009, Page 9A

Auto repair shops opened in early 1900s

Transition from Blacksmith Shops to Automotive Repair Shops

After the 19th century, blacksmithing was slowly becoming a profession of the past because of the technological advancement of the automotive industry. Blacksmithing prior to the era mentioned had assumed the responsibility of shoeing mules or horses, repairing or fabricating farm implements (plows, harrows, scoop-pans, seed-planters), horse drawn carriages/wagons and repairing machinery at grainmills or sawmills.

There were several blacksmiths of notoriety in Northwest Orange County; namely Gustav Loeffler, S. W. Eldredge, George Bleh, Henry Terrell, William Ohse, and Beverly W. Hull. Some stood out in their trade well into the 1950s.

Around 1909, several purchases of automobiles begin to surface and continued into the World War I era. Supposedly, James Dean's proprietorship was one of the earliest auto service stations in Apopka. According to records in 1920, Widrig and Jackson, proprietors of the Apopka Hardware Store, annexed a garage to service automobiles that became Chevrolet's and Studebaker's agency for repairs.

Later, under different ownership, a franchise was obtained to service and sell the Hanson automobile. John Jackson, after a few years of successful automotive services, sold the previously mentioned business to Dwight Risener and R. A. Lasater. Lasater, at that point in time, had gained notoriety as being one of the top mechanics in Apopka. In approximately 1922, a Ford franchise dealer, Dan Vaden, opened a business on U.S. Highway 441 in Apopka. Around 1922, Cato Sanders of Negro heritage opened his service station on Ninth Street and South Central Avenue, becoming the first service station in the "project" area. E. E. Trask, an agent for Standard Oil, and Clement H. Womble's Gulf Oil distributorship supplied fuel for the area's trucks and automobiles.

Al Davis was an entrepreneur and a prominent, renowned, competent mechanic in the area. It was noted that the majority of his ex-employees, who were mechanics, would eventually seek the endeavors of auto parts dealer proprietorship.

Slim recalls, during the 1940s prior to E. J. King's proprietorship of his auto parts enterprise, his endeavors involved being the number one iceman for the Apopka Ice Company, along with being a part-time mechanic at Al Davis' Garage. Around 1950, E. J. King established an auto parts dealership in the old Samuel Eldredge Livery building at Main Street and Central Avenue. King's business prospered to the extent that it was necessary to relocate into a larger facility to accommodate parts, precision rebuilding machines, and additional customer parking that was located near the old Midland Railroad historic turntable of yesteryear on Third Street between Forest and Highland avenues.

14 Service Station first Lasater's Automotive & Aircraft Garage and then known as King's Auto Parts. Photo AHS.

E. J. worked well into the 20th century to build a business of renowned reputation as King's Auto

Parts. Presently, his grandson Dan, whom he tutored in business practices for many years, has assumed complete control of King's Auto Parts.

Fred Joiner, in the 1950s, along with his Massey-Ferguson tractor dealership and repair garage, initiated a renowned auto parts department at the dealership. Joiner's enterprises remained stable until the closing of the muck farms around the area and the devastating freezes (1970s-1980s) that decimated many of the local crop and vegetation areas. After the failure of his repair business due to the farming failures in the area, Fred pursued raising hogs in Hawkinsville, Georgia.

The Apopka Chief, July 3, 2009, Page 9A

Civil Defense was alive and well in the Apopka area during WWII

World War II Condition--Hardships Encountered

In a past edition of *The Apopka Chief* newspaper, the illustrious botanist of this area and era, namely, Jack Christmas, who is also a weekly columnist producing the "Historical Tidbits" column, penned an interesting article pertaining to World War II incidents that occurred in the small communities of Northwest Orange County. This article reminded me vividly of that moment in time. However, Jack, with your permission, Slim hopes he can piggyback onto your article with a few additions of occurrences (smile) that he is familiar with.

Although the United States of America has been involved in two major wars after the U.S. Civil War (1861-1865), none have been fought upon United States soil other than the Civil War. World War II, during its presence in Europe and the Pacific, made America extremely aware of protecting its borders and infrastructures, thus creating numerous means of protective innovations to offset disastrous consequences employed by the enemy.

The Civil Defense Project was created as a means of preventive measures against enemy attacks. Carl Jackson was selected to head this program for Northwest Orange County. He was nurtured and attended public schools in the Apopka area many years prior to WWII.

Jackson, as an adult, was involved in several business enterprises along with the constant appetite for civic matters. He served as an Orange County Commissioner from 1933-1941. The Civil Defense Project in this area was comprised of Apopka Police Chief Fred Risener, F. L. Burgust of State Bank of Apopka, and Mayor Ted Waite and they implemented procedures and planning relative to probable attacks.

Fred Risener, chief air raid warden, also appointed Sam "Bubber" Weaver as an air raid warden who resided below the TO&A Railroad tracks for that area. Slim recalls two complete blackouts issued by Chief Risener, wherein most citizens living in the prescribed area heretofore-mentioned assembled at Ninth Street (Michael Gladden) and South Central Avenue (meanwhile no lights or smoking) awaiting the siren signal for all clear. The air raid warden assigned to the previously mentioned area stressed the point of totally following the procedures whenever occasional mock Civil Defense drills were issued. He often went door-to-door verbalizing the circumstances rather than utilizing the siren that notified citizens of an imminent attack.

At this point in time in the early part of 1942, Estelle King of Zellwood was in charge of the rationing board that issued ration stamps pertaining to commodities, and she had offices located in Apopka and Zellwood.

Restrictions on commodities were enforced with the introduction of a limited quantity of ration stamps for obtaining goods such as coffee, sugar, shoes, and gasoline. In relation to gasoline, automobile windshields had decals (A-B-C-D) placed onto them and these letters denoted the number of gallons one would receive when purchasing gasoline. The rationing board was comprised of John Ustler and E. W. Fly, as well as R. T. Carlton, who handled vehicle tires.

During the WWII years, American citizens responded to adverse situations tremendously with the hope that victory was imminent.

By the way, Jack, Slim reads and is enlightened by your column each and every week, and again, Slim thanks you for letting me piggyback on this one. Thanks Jack!

World War II
Second World War
September 1, 1939—September 2, 1945

Olmstead Publishing LLC

The Apopka Chief, July 10, 2009, Page 14A

Black businesses thrived in Apopka area

Early Negro Businesses in Northwest Orange County – Apopka, Tangerine, Clarcona, Zellwood and Plymouth

Several years ago, during Ms. Mildred A. Board's tenure as a columnist for Bits 'n' Tips in *The Apopka Chief* weekly newspaper, she requested that Slim pen a reference to Negro businesses in Northwest Orange County. This article was to delve into the premise that most entrepreneurs of that era and ethnicity relied upon their respective businesses for their livelihood to support their families and other financial obligations. At one point in time, there were approximately 75 different forms of owned and operated black businesses in the area. It is Slim's intentions in this particular penning to be brief as to naming all or most of the 75 entrepreneurs; therefore, if anyone is omitted, it was not intentional, but Slim knew that article would be lengthy, precipitating a second episode (smile).

By coincidence, Slim was privileged to meet and converse with a very talented, sincere, inspiring, conscientious, educated, entrepreneurial young person by the name of Mrs. Theresa Baldwin Mott, who was nurtured here in Apopka attended Phyllis Wheatley School, Apopka High School and Seminole Community College, majoring in business administration. Presently, Theresa operates a business in Apopka on SR 436, adjacent to the Department of Motor Vehicles and has so for several years. Her interest in our ethnicity's businesses of the past and present, along with our white counterparts, precipitated through Theresa's involvement with the Apopka Area Chamber of Commerce. Secondly, her parents were among some of the early Negro settlers in the 1900s in Apopka who migrated from Alabama seeking employment, homes, sharecropping and business endeavors (farming, cattle and horse breeding, blacksmithing).

Theresa B. Mott's constant inquiries of her ethnicity's past and present business interests, along with their other achievements, precipitated Slim penning this article relative to the period of time initiating approximately before and shortly after the United States of America's Civil War in 1865.

There were several white slave owners with six or more slaves in the Northwest Orange County area, namely William C. Goolsby, James R. Stewart, and Matthew Bryan. William S. Delk, who was from the area, also owned more slaves than his neighbors from 1845-1865. Delk, who had migrated from Georgia, was somewhat of an environmentalist who utilized the natural resources of the Rock Springs Run area to promote sawmilling techniques, basic farming practices, turpentine harvesting and grainmilling, making Delk the leading entrepreneur during his tenure until his demise in 1885.

American Civil War
War Between the States
Shot-to-Shot
April 12, 1861—June 22, 1865
By Declaration
January 1861—May 9, 1865

Shortly after the Civil War ended in 1865, the majority of owners freed their slaves due to the economic crisis because the owners were not able to financially own slaves and maintain their lands. Therefore, some owners allowed the freed slaves to remain on their farms or current industry that they owned. According to records, many of the slaves migrated into Lake County in and around Sorrento near Rock Springs Run. This migration led Joseph G. Roberts, a slave of Negro heritage, who claimed

© 2015

William S. Delk to be his natural father by a Negro maid slave he had owned, along with many others, to move into Seminole County.

Mainly because it was the St. Johns River's gateway to most interior portions of Florida, families, adventurers, entrepreneurs, speculators and investors tended to migrate to enhance the probability of an ex-slave to obtain gainful employment, and a place of refuge. Another focal point of entry or exit during this era that interested ex-slaves and freepersons included the Lake Apopka chain of lakes that connected to the Oklawaha River, which was navigable to shallow draft boats for waterway transportation. This brought goods and people creating the probability of a livelihood which most had not experienced under bondage.

This area was vast in size and inhabited by only a few white settlers on both sides of Lake Apopka. Nevertheless, Indians of the Seminole Timucuan tribe, known as the Acuera, along with numerous Negroes (freed or ex-slaves) who lived among the Indians, maintained their livelihood by trading, hunting, fishing and camping mainly on the eastern shores of Lake Apopka lasting into the 1850s (climax of the Seminole Wars).

Shortly after the American Civil War, railroad construction became very prevalent, according to official census records. This led to the opportunity for hundreds of Negro ex-slaves to be hired to build tracks throughout Florida for commercial and passenger transportation. With such an influx of railroad workers, many decided to remain in the area pursuing railroad construction or take up residency within the area.

A Negro railroad worker named Steven Hooper, hired during this construction era, according to United States Census Records (1880), remained in the Apopka area and amassed a substantial amount of property between Merrimack and Rock Springs Run in and around 1870, according to the Orange County Book of Records. Ms. Francina Boykin, a member of the Apopka Historical Society, has in her possession that particular legal document with artifacts pertaining to Negro ownership history in Apopka. The Steven Hooper family, who happens to be of Negro ethnicity, at one point in time, owned more property than anyone of their race in Apopka.

In the 1870s, there were two distinct areas where coloreds resided in Apopka, one being Johnson Town (Lake Avenue and Oak Street) and the other, Sarah Mead's Bottom near The Lodge.

In the late 1870s, an entrepreneur of Negro heritage, namely Sarah Mead, appeared on the scene in an area then called by the pioneers Sarah Mead's Bottom, shortly after which she homesteaded in the area.

15 Francina Boykin in her one-woman show depicting Sarah Mead at a meeting of the Apopka Historical Society. Dr.O. 2011 06 11

Sarah migrated from Jacksonville, where she established a network with her sister to recruit families, adventurers, farmers, and other individuals to obtain property. These were people who were interested in some form of livelihood, such as the area's production of agriculture products, sawmilling, turpentine distilling and railroad construction. These individuals and families were the primary support of her business enterprises, which entailed stable renting, shanty shotgun houses for rent, commissary, and in some cases, to act as a mediator between the powers that be.

George Oden, an individual of color, was a competent, renowned citrus caretaker in and around the latter 1890s. This period was a noted citrus recovery period after the devastating freezes of 1894-1895. Mr. Oden contributed to the community in several arenas by maintaining roadways, right-of-ways and donating property (i.e. the property for the construction of the present day New Hope Missionary Baptist Church at South Central Avenue and Tenth Street). Around 1912, a gigantic lightning strike on the old original church located in Mead's Bottom caused destruction of the structure due to a massive fire. Oden gained notoriety in the 1900s, when he purchased a forty-acre bearing citrus grove near the Marshal Lake chain of lakes flowing into Lake Apopka. A purchase of this magnitude was highly unusual for a person of color during that era.

16 New Hope Missionary Baptist Church. Photo Dr.O. 2014 12 29

Ella Walls, also of Negro ethnicity, owned property and a home near the Amos D. Starbird sons' Consumers Lumber & Veneer Company sawmill. At the time, Ella, was able to obtain slab lumber free by just asking. These slabs suited the purpose of constructing shanty shotgun houses that influenced her to enter the rental housing entrepreneurship, which she turned into a lucrative enterprise. Many of the colored employees at CL&VC sawmill. At the time, Ella were in need of housing accommodations along with the many newcomers to the area and they usually rented these facilities from Mrs. Walls. Late into the 1960s, several of those houses still remained standing and occupied.

Olmstead Publishing LLC

Cato Sanders, a person of color, arrived in the area around the turn of the 19th century from North Carolina seeking a better livelihood in Florida. Cato, prior coming to Florida, was a blacksmith. S. Eldredge, a prominent proprietor of several enterprises, hired Sanders as a blacksmith in addition to being livery service driver whenever drummers requested transportation for the purpose of promoting goods, taking orders on products to be delivered at a later date and selling goods throughout the area. Cato Sanders was the first of his race to construct and own an automotive repair and service station on South Central Avenue and Ninth Street (nowadays Michael Gladden Blvd.) around the 1920s.

Henry Terrell was another blacksmith of Negro heritage who migrated into Tangerine during the period when blacksmithing was an absolute necessity due to the transition from blacksmith shops to automobile service station. Terrell shod horses and mules, as well as repaired farm implements and animal drawn carriages/wagons that brought him into notoriety as a competent blacksmith in Lake and Orange counties. Presently, there is a roadway in Tangerine named Terrell Road in his honor.

The majority of Negro families who could not financially afford prenatal care or birthing fees at hospitals constantly utilized midwives during the early 1900s into the 1950s. These people depended upon three professional competent, renowned individuals of color to assist in the birthing process, namely Mrs. Epsie Williams of Clarcona, Mrs. Pickett of Mead's Bottom, and Mrs. Rosa Barnes of Old Clarcona Road in Apopka who was sanctioned by the beloved Dr. Thomas "Tommy" McBride, M.D. and his medical predecessors.

Jooks below the TO&A Railroad tracks was initiated in the late teens and early 1920s by a Negro, Richard "Dick" Hayward, who was the "granddaddy of jooks." Hayward was from the "swamp fox" state that is named for the famous American Revolutionary War general, Francis Marion of South Carolina. Between the 1910s and 1920s, and to some degree, even today, jooks have a tendency to be a way of ethnic entertainment in "Soulsville." Dick's original jook remained operational under his proprietorship into the late 1940s.

Lemuel Board, the biological father of former columnist Mildred A. Board, arrived in the Apopka area in the early 1900s from the blue grass state of

Kentucky, bringing his business of horse training and breeding into Apopka.

In the 1930s and continuing into the 1970s, Negro proprietors of businesses below the TO&A Railroad tracks organized an association that undertook the responsibility of the landscape maintenance and sales of grave space at the Apopka Colored Cemetery, as it was known then. During that forty-year period of time, the association purchased additional property adjacent to the existing Apopka Colored Cemetery from Dr. Thomas E. "Tommy" McBride. Shortly thereafter, the members of the association unanimously agreed to speak to the City of Apopka in regards to the city assuming complete ownership, management, and maintenance of the Apopka Colored Cemetery. The association, in addition to relinquishing all property rights, gave the City of Apopka a complete detailed diagram drawing of Apopka Colored Cemetery area, submitted on brown butcher's meat wrapping paper from M. Gladden's Groceries. This drawing of the Apopka Colored Cemetery indicated all of the grave lot spaces. Last but not least, negotiating via a handshake agreement, the association gave all monies held in the association coffers to the City of Apopka without any restraints.

Mrs. Theresa B. Mott! Hopefully, Slim has given you a small insight regarding businesses and achievements of our heritage over the past hundred years or so. Slim was indeed fortunate to meet and converse with numerous reputable black and white figures that inspired Slim's concern with this area's business and achievement history.

Two individuals of different ethnicity, the Honorable Mayor John H. Land and longtime Apopka entrepreneur Michael Gladden Jr., should receive most of the credit for this article, being they were thoroughly informed by responsible individuals, documentation records kept privately and experiences involvement in politics and businesses.

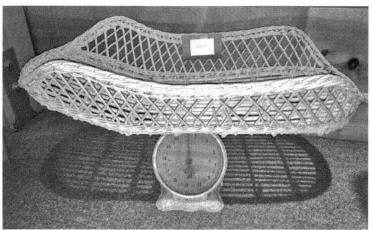

17 This infant scale used by Dr. Thomas McBride is at the Museum of the Apopkans. Many an Apopkan graced this scale. Photo by DrO 2015.

The Pennings of Perrine Slim

The Apopka Chief, July 24, 2009, Page 11A

Apopka principals were dedicated

A Tribute to OCPS Principals of the 1930s to 1950s

This article reflects upon the Orange County Public Schools system during the 1930s-1950s, from which great results have been achieved through tremendous struggles. Most principals of Negro heritage during that era are in Jehovah God's hand. From this rare breed of educators, only three were noted among society in the late 1990s and early 21st century–Cecil Boston, Marie Stapler Gladden and Frank M. Otey. Several months ago, Otey's and Boston's demise occurred.

18 Marie S. Gladden and her first class in Sanford 1923.
Photo from Francina Boykin.

Marie S. Gladden, the last of the big three principals, passed away May 14, 2004 at the age of 100.

Other educators of color, who also served as principals, C. W. Jennings, Edith H. Williams, Banks, Ms. Dixon-Sanders, Mr. Manigualt, Ms. Flakes, Mr. Maxey, Ms. Hall, and G. W. Fort, were all well qualified academically to hold the office of principal for OCPS at any level and did so with much excellence, despite limited resources and political encroachment. They had a unique and important role in educating students to cope with 20th and 21st century ideals and issues.

Jobs educating pupils are extremely difficult, and demanding, among other things, public relations, parental surrogate, administrator, utilizing personal funds for students' academic purposes, motivator, and confessor. When you delve into those records of what some of these pupils they tutored accomplished, you will be astonished as to their achievements.

During that span of time, numerous students went on to excel in many avenues of constructive endeavors, such as teaching (secondary education and college), politics, and military (rank of full colonel). Several excelled in vocational specialties, including engineering, medicine, dentistry, theology, agriculture, jurisprudence, master musician, law enforcement (federal and state), scientific research (ades egypti), sports (National Football League, Negro Baseball league – Indianapolis Clowns, St. Louis Cardinal minor league baseball team and Florida high school board member).

Their leadership, precipitated by their role model opportunities, was a catalyst in most pupils' development of character and accomplishments. On behalf of all students, including Slim, of that era during the "good old days," we thank you special individuals very much for your persistence, effort, time, concern, compassion, understanding and instilling into students that the future is a glance away if pupils have the initiative to strive for it.

There are so many wonderful opportunities awaiting your grasp.

The Apopka Chief, July 31, 2009, Page 13A

After years of delivering mail, carrier spends his time at the tree

Mail Carrier in Apopka

Most citizens favorably call Willie Lewis Freeman "Government" or "Mailman" as Freeman was known relative to his job description as a U.S. postal carrier throughout every neighborhood in the Apopka area.

Freeman was nurtured in Orange County and attended Phyllis Wheatley Elementary and Phyllis Wheatley High School, graduating in 1968. He was a member of one of the two remaining senior high school classes to graduate from PWHS prior to the high school phase being eliminated.

Upon completing his academic studies, Freeman was employed by the Florida Roads Maintenance Department for several years prior to entering into the U.S. Air Force.

When the U.S. Postal Service initially hired Freeman, approximately some forty years ago, mail carriers walked the entire route door to door with a leather over-the-shoulder bag, placing letters or packages at prescribed facilities according to their addresses.

However, as the quantity of mail increased, it became necessary for the carriers to pick up mail from centralized mailboxes in an area to complete delivery throughout their route.

Walking door to door became a thing of the past due to innovation of mailboxes that served all addresses in a prescribed block where recipients could pick up their mail rather than have it delivered door to door. This increase in the amount of mail also precipitated the utilization of bicycles and jeep-style trucks for the carrier to transport mail to designated areas.

Nowadays, "Government" spends a considerable portion of his leisure time at the "tree" (Michael Gladden Blvd and Central Ave.) conversing with senior citizens and numerous passersby about politics, civic issues, academic issues, racial ramifications and economics. There have been numerous incidents in which Government temporarily addressed circumstances other than postal service to assist a citizen in distress.

Slim's curiosity heightens whenever conversing with Mailman in regards to his knowledge about and experiences with the average citizen of Apopka, whether he or she lives above or below the TO&A Railroad tracks over the forty-year span of time.

For years, Freeman has had a keen interest in antique automobiles as to their preservation and ownership. Upon graduation in 1968, he acquired a

1957 Buick to commute to a workshop in Oviedo. At one point in time, he acquired two antique vehicles that had to be noticed whenever they passed by.

Willie Lewis Freeman! Slim and hundreds of citizens of this area extend their appreciation for the services you have continuously performed, even nowadays, without reservations about time, location, or adverse weather conditions. Government, Mailman, Freeman and all those other names we use to refer to you, "We wholeheartedly thank you."

Former NFL player works for city

Homegrown Politician Nurtured in
Apopka on Blueberry Hill

Slim had the opportunity to converse with this aspiring, unique, conscientious, compassionate, concerned and caring young man, Rogers Beckett Jr., prior to his graduation from Apopka High School more than a decade ago.

My encounters with Rogers Jr. precipitated from being advised of his constant desire to achieve with excellence pertaining to academics, especially during his tenure at Apopka High School, along with being a superb football athlete.

The majority of his family members, friends and acquaintances favorably called Rogers Beckett Jr. "Red" during most of his nurturing in Apopka. Therefore, Slim will, at some point in time during this penning, utilize that alias whenever deemed necessary.

Rogers Beckett Jr. excelled as a pupil and athlete in all phases of education (primary, secondary, and college) periods from 1983 through 1995 while attending Phyllis Wheatley Elementary School, Apopka Memorial Middle School and graduating from Apopka High School in 1995.

© 2015

His athleticism and academic achievements prompted numerous higher educational institutions (Appalachian College, Oklahoma and Marshall College) to recruit him as a scholarship student athlete.

Red repeated his excellence in academics and athletics at Marshall College in Huntington, West Virginia, from 1995 to 1999, receiving a bachelor of science degree. Upon graduating he was invited to participate in the National Football League's compound evaluation camp to determine if Red's athleticism was sufficient to perform as a professional football player. His skills caught the attention of several NFL teams who desperately needed a player for the safety position that Red was capable of playing with absolute authority.

The San Diego Chargers selected him as their first draft choice of the second round in 1999.

He was able to start playing immediately with success. After spending a few years playing on the first string as a defensive back, Red was traded to the Cincinnati Bengals. In his second season as a Bengal, he sustained a head injury, and several physicians advised him that the next concussion probably would be serious beyond rehabilitation.

At this point in time, through constant talks with his father Rogers "Hawk" Beckett, Sr. about continuing as an NFL player, they concurred with several physicians rather than risk permanent head injury, so Red retired.

Most conversations Slim has had with Beckett Jr. in recent years pertained to a social scientist's viewpoint regarding mankind's perception of life in general. He has definitely found his niche in becoming a vital portion of Apopka's community development organization. Since his tenure with the City of Apopka Community Development Department, there have been considerable noticeable changes, especially constructive programs for juveniles and young individuals that serve as a catalyst to strengthen their future growth in becoming a person of value to themselves and society. Recently, Red's participation in these community meetings has shown that the City of Apopka is willing to address the needs and issues for all areas of this quaint, petite community of Apopka.

Slim, along with numerous concerned citizens, thanks you for your interest in humankind's potential development.

Apopka firefighter is active in his community

An Apopka Firefighter

Slim, on numerous occasions, has had the opportunity and privilege to meet and converse with this 21st century firefighter of black heritage, Bobby "B. J." Scott, about policies and procedures regarding his profession with unlimited details. These encounters with B. J. were precipitated by many years of conversations prior to him becoming a firefighter that Slim had with the illustrious former fire chief, Leroy "Roy" Gilliam, the granddaddy of Apopka firefighters. He was responsible for establishing the Apopka Fire Department and departments in the surrounding rural areas of Northwest Orange County (policies, procedures, accessible water hydrants, firefighting equipment). These actions were initiated in the mid-20th century with many of Chief Gilliam's innovations being employed even in the early 21st century.

As of this penning in July 2009, let it be noted that B.J. Scott is the oldest active fireman age-wise (58 years) currently employed by the Orange County Fire Department.

B. J. Scott was the first black student to graduate from Apopka High School with a basketball scholarship during mandatory integration, and he is a Lake-Sumter Community College alumni. He has served 10 years as an Orlando professional firefighter and 20 years as an Orange County professional firefighter.

Bobby is currently active in the annual Relay For Life event, Men of the South Apopka Community Club; active member of St. Paul AME Church (church steward, finance officer and president of church men's club), and Progressive Firefighters Association (black firefighters' union) throughout the U.S.A.

Slim, along with many citizens of Orange County; certainly appreciate the services you have rendered, regardless of life threatening circumstances. Thank you, B. J. Scott.

The Apopka Chief, September 11, 2009, Page 13A

Apopka has its share of sports stars

Home Grown Professional Athletes of the Apopka Area--Baseball and Football Sandlot Players Initiating in the 20th Century

Recently, in an edition of *The Apopka Chief* weekly newspaper, the famous renowned, competent botanist Jack Christmas, the former proprietor of Oakdell Nursery of the Apopka-Plymouth area, wrote about the interest in and the importance of baseball for the entire community uptown and downtown during 1920s through 1940s.

At that point in time, baseball was almost a religion among Apopka citizens (smile). It was during that era that the king of all sports was, without a doubt, baseball!!

Apparently, there is a mystique within the air, water, and sands in the Apopka area that tends to elevate individuals to perform and master their profession of athleticism in a designated field of their choice.

Slim has had the opportunity to converse and play with individuals who ascertained that plateau of sports professionalism. Some of Apopka's citizens, not of Slim's ethnicity, were indeed superb athletes, especially in the 1920-1940 eras.

They brought prestige, notoriety, and publicity for Apopka and themselves when they eventually became professional baseball players in the major leagues; namely, Robert G. Pitman Jr., Harold McCormick and George "Jug" Anderson.

Slim had the privilege to meet on several occasions with Robert G. Pitman Jr., after his stint with the major leagues. Lee Neil Sr., of colored heritage and a renowned superb baseball player, quite frequently practiced privately hitting one on one with Pitman.

The Apopka Colored Baseball Team, below the TO&A Railroad tracks during that period in history, accumulated players capable of professional major league status, but the opportunity for black players was not to come until approximately ten years later. However, Raymond Neil, prior to the National and American major league's acceptance of persons of color in the early 1940s, was acquired in the 1940s by the professional Negro Baseball League (Indianapolis Clowns), who were capable of competing with its white counterparts in leagues whenever the opportunity presented itself.

Nevertheless, Raymond Neil played for 15 years with Indianapolis before being given a tryout for the majors, but by that time, his age precipitated rejection. Louis "Nick" Garvin, a "soul brother" and Apopka-nurtured lad, excelled in all three basic sports (baseball, football, basketball) throughout secondary school and while attending college at Shaw University in North Carolina. Upon graduation in the late 1950's the St. Louis Cardinals of the National Baseball League acquired Garvin for their AAA Club as a shortstop.

Jeremi Rudolph, of black heritage, graduated from Apopka High School in 1995 and was a very versatile athlete in football and baseball. However, major league baseball scouts from the Kansas City Royals became interested in acquiring his commitments to their system immediately after completing his secondary education and placed him in their farm system in Florida. He participated for approximately one-and-a-half years, until he sustained a severe shoulder injury, thus diminishing his baseball career.

Zack Grienke, an Apopka High School graduate and, potentially, a very talented pitcher was highly recruited by numerous major league baseball teams, but the Kansas City Royals obtained the draft rights for him.

Zack's tenure within the minor leagues was brief due to his pitching ability, thus thrusting him into the majors after less than one year, moving him from the Florida minor league to the Kansas City Royals.

On July 14, Grienke pitched in the fourth inning of the Major League All-Stars Game in St. Louis for the American League combatants versus National League.

[Editors addendum for Greinke since original composition:
Kansas City Royals (2004–2010)
Milwaukee Brewers (2011–2012)
Los Angeles Angels of Anaheim (2012)
Los Angeles Dodgers (2013–present)
Career highlights and awards
2 time Baseball All-Star (2009, 2014)
MLB ERA leader (2009)
AL Cy Young Award (2009)
Gold Glove Award (2014)
Silver Slugger Award (2013)]

As for the "pigskin" professionals that were nurtured in Northwest Orange County, their athleticism denotes attention throughout this wonderful unique world of Jehovah God. Many players of different ethnicity have made their mark in the arena of professional football.

They are listed with their college and professional football affiliation:

Aaron Jones, Eastern Kentucky University, Pittsburgh Steelers, New England Patriots, [Miami Dolphins];

Brandon Meriweather, University of Miami (UM), New England Patriots, Chicago Bears, Washington Redskins;

Brent [Robert] Bartholomew, Ohio State, Miami Dolphins, Chicago Bears, [Washington Redskins];

Chris Shepherd, Florida Atlantic University (FAU), Atlanta Falcons;

David McMillian Jr. University of Kansas, Cleveland Browns;

Derrick [Lee] Clark, Evangel College, Denver Broncos;

Dimitrius Breedlove, Evangel College, Cleveland Browns;

Doug [Lee] Kellom, University of Florida (UF), Canadian League;

Eddie Williams, UM, New York Giants;

James [Edward] McKnight, Liberty University, Seattle Seahawks, Miami Dolphins, Dallas Cowboys;

Joe Calloway, Birmingham Stallions;

Kent Elmore, University of Tennessee, Los Angeles Rams;

Kris Comstock, University of Kentucky, [Cleveland Browns];

Mark Murray, UF, Denver Broncos;

Mark Selig, University of Miami;

Melvin Jones, Livingston University, Denver Broncos training camp;

Sammie Smith, Florida Sate University (FSU), Miami Dolphins, Denver Broncos;

Warren Sapp, UM, Tampa Bay Buccaneers, Oakland Raiders;

Willie Hughley, Florida International University (FIU), Cincinnati Bengals.

Slim, along with many other citizens, thank you, professional players, for your efforts and the emotional feeling we as fans ascertain from seeing you perform.

[Editor: More Noteable Sports Figures, provided by Melvin Jones and Editor's Research]

Football

Greg Thompson, FSU, Coach Southern A&M, Morris Brown, Clark Atlanta, St. Clair

Jacquian Williams, University of South Florida (USF), New York Giants

Jaye Howard, UF, Seattle Seahawks

Jeremi Rudolph, University of Las Vegas, (went pro baseball)

Jonathan Dwight Edge, University of Tampa, (went pro baseball)

Kyle Wilber, Wake Forest, Dallas Cowboys

Larry Lumpkin, Alabama A&M/Carson-Newman, Indianapolis Colts

Mike Lowman, Coffeyville Community College, Dallas Cowboys draft

Robert Drummond, Syracuse, Philidelphia Eagles

Rodney Brewer, UF, (went pro baseball)

Rogers Beckett, Marshall University, San Diego Chargers, Cincinatti Bengals

Baseball

Brett King, USF, San Francisco Giants Minors
Charles E. Williams, Bailtimore Orioles Minors
Chris DeClue, Flagler College
Jeremi Rudolph, Toronto Blue Jays, Medicine Hats, Minors
Jonathan DeClue, Florida Southern College, California Angels Minors, Houston Astros Minors
Jonathan Dwight Edge, University of Tampa, Arizona Diamondbacks, Pittsburgh Pirates, Oakland Athletes Minors
Keith E. Fisher, Bristol Tigers, Detroit Tigers Macon Peaches Minors
Rodney Brewer, UF, St Louis Cardinals Minors

Track and Field

Sammie Lee Smith, FSU, (went pro football)

19 Sammie Smith training Deion Luwynn Sanders in Track and Field at Florida State. Photo by Christopher Holder.

Olmstead Publishing LLC

20 Twins, Jonathan and Chris DeClue, Apopka baseball standouts now insurance business owners, CF Insurance Services, Inc. Photo DeClue brothers.

The Apopka Chief, October 2, 2009, Page 10A

Mules were useful back in the day

Usage of Mules--Modern Day Innovations and Technology has Curtailed Usage of Mules

These hybrids (the offspring of parents that are of different species or strains) between the domestic horse and the donkey do not occur in a wild state, but have been developed by domestic breeding. The breeding of mules began in ancient times, probably in Asia Minor, and the animals were brought to Greece at a very early period. They were frequently mentioned by numerous writers, namely Homer, Hesiod, Theognis, and others of that point in time, and held in high esteem for their superior strength.

From Greece, they were introduced into ancient Italy wherein they became very popular for hauling carts on the highways in Varro's time (poet, *circa*100 B.C.), much as they do in the region today. From Rome, they became widely diffused in Europe, and the Latin names "mulus" and "hinnus" were adopted into languages of most people who made use of these hybrids, translating into the English names, "mule" and "hinny," at the present day.

21 **Mules and alligators were signs of the times in the pioneering days of Apopka. View at the Museum of the Apopkans.**

The mule is the only hybrid among domesticated animals that has risen to true economic importance and worldwide use. Despite its sullen disposition and its notoriety of being much less affectionate than the horse, it possesses a high degree of intelligence. The finest mules are reared in Spain and the United States of America. Once a year, in Columbia, Tennessee (Maury County), a festival is held pertaining to the state's special breeding of mules along with honoring mules for their contributions to society.

Also, Montana is famous for its extraordinary breeding of good mules, better known as the "Montana Mule." In the 1800s, as the United States expanded especially in the west, this encouraged mankind to explore and settle the far western states and led to the conception of the famous 20-mule teams, due to the animals' endurance and strength as they crossed areas similar to Death Valley, transporting goods, supplies and equipment.

This article was conceived through constant thoughts of Slim's past experiences and conversations relative to mules and men below the TO&A Railroad tracks in Apopka, initiating with Orange County resident George Oden of Negro heritage from Talladega County, Alabama. Being employed in the 19th century by the famous Cogswell Citrus Groves of Lakeville precipitated Oden's interest, persistence, and training for numerous years in citrus grove service procedures. He became a renowned, competent citrus grove service entrepreneur from 1890-1939, and at that point in time, he owned several mules, which were very significant to Oden's citrus endeavors and livelihood.

22 Josephine and Bennett Land @1918. Source Stephen Nelson

Documented records can substantiate that, after Oden's demise in 1939, the Consumers Lumber & Veneer Company of Apopka, then owned by the Bennett Land family, agreed to purchase two of his mules from the Oden's estate. Sam "Parson" Small Sr., a native of South Carolina, arrived in Apopka in the late 1890s, bringing his experiences and expertise of vegetable farming. He then purchased seven acres north of the present-day sites of the City of Apopka's water recharge area on the north side of Cleveland Street, adjoining Highland Avenue on the east side.

Sam Sr., utilized mules he owned for his farming activities. In addition, he used mules for pulling conventional style wagons for transportation of farming implements and produce within Apopka. Slim recalls constantly seeing him and his wife ride aboard the single mule-drawn, four-wheeled wagon as a form of transportation to and from church services and other activities.

George Girtman, a Negro, purchased farmland in the southeast section of Tilden's Addition in Apopka during the early 20th century for vegetable farming and a variety of citrus trees that he maintained with mules. Even today, some of his offspring reside on the existing property but no mules (smile).

"Old Man Turner," a person of color who was an entrepreneur with ventures, such as producing vegetable farming products, charcoal production and sugarcane grinding. In these cases, mules were extremely significant in each in the aforementioned projects. Turner lived south of Girtman, below the TO&A Railroad tracks.

Will Huffman, a brother of color originally from Alachua County, arrived in Apopka in the 1920s and resided on East 12th Street near South Robinson Avenue. Huffman owned several mules that he utilized relative to agriculture ventures for years.

Often Slim, nowadays, reflects upon the few men in the latter 20th century who are the last people owning and utilizing mules on a daily basis whenever requested. Ossie Cannon, a soul brother, was an employee of the Honorable Mayor John H. Land at the CL&VC for many years as a driver-operator of two-wheeled, mule-drawn wagons utilized by the yard. Daily, Ossie traveled to Bennett Land Sr.'s estate (Alabama Avenue and Sixth Street) from the mill site to perform duties of milking goats and gathering eggs in addition to feeding and watering goats, guineas and chickens under the watchful eyes of the grand matriarch, Mrs. Josephine Land.

Once the mill closed, he purchased mules to establish his own proprietorship of mules for hire in citrus and foliage nurseries, in addition to cultivation of small acreage plots. Constantly, you would observe Ossie aboard his single mule-drawn, four-wheeled wagon loaded with cultivating implements with another mule tied behind the wagon, heading north on Park Avenue toward the Merrimack and Bay Ridge areas.

This method of utilizing two mules for the work at hand decreased the burden of fatigue on just one mule, especially whenever traveling several miles to designated work areas.

Maxwell Howard, a person of colored heritage, ventured into Apopka around the early 1940s, pursuing his dreams of farming. Eventually, he met Mr. Harris of the same ethnicity, who owned farmland near Lake Apopka (Binion Road), where they participated in vegetable farming practices along with citrus growing.

At this point in time, Maxwell owned mules for hire. He would transport his farming implements on the back of a pickup truck to the designated site, with the mule tied to rear of pickup truck, moving at a slow pace so the mule would not break a natural walking gait. Apparently, Mr. Howard never trained his mules to be bodily transported on the truck.

Willie Long, of colored ethnicity, owned mules and did odd jobs that were extremely dependent on the mule's performance pertaining to vegetable farming or breaking new ground. His mules, by themselves, were frequently seen visiting Ossie Cannon's mules on South Robinson Avenue and East 11th Street, whenever they broke out of Longs' stable over on West 14th Street near Central Avenue.

Although mules are rarely seen nowadays, they, along with the men that handled them, shall not be forgotten. "Whoa, mule! Now git!"(smile, smile).

In closing, Slim had the privilege of meeting and conversing with all of these "muleskinners," beginning with the renowned Mr. George Oden.

The Apopka Chief, October 16, 2009, Page 14A

Linda Lee is a concerned citizen

National Night Out Against Crime and Empowering Youth to Block Out Crime

For numerous years, Ms. Linda Lee, a person of colored ethnicity, has been one of the very active concerned citizens in reference to crime activity below the TO&A Railroad tracks.

She was nurtured in Apopka on Clarcona Road and East 15th Street. She initiated her academic career at Phyllis Wheatley Elementary School and completed the secondary phase of her education at Hungerford High School in Eatonville.

Ms. Linda's visions pertaining to youth blocking out crime stemmed from her involvement with the Village House programs for youth at her home in late 20th century into the 21st century. For the past three years (2007-2009), Ms. Lee has been extremely significant in organizing National Night Out Against Crime in the 15th Street area of Apopka.

During the first two years of National Night Out Against Crime, Ms. Linda absorbed the majority of the financial responsibility on her own. However, in 2009, the membership of her church, Progressive Holiness Freewill Church of Apopka, Macedonia Free Methodist Church (Pastor Calvin Ashley) of

Apopka, and a few concerned citizens, along with an agency representing programs of this type, assisted with financial contributions.

Approximately 150 persons of different ages and ethnicity were in attendance. The program agenda selected for this year described those overwhelming negative issues youth must not and will not abide by in order to block out crime. Speakers Shanta Mitchell Holmes, former tutor at the Village House, Rev. Gerald Moss of Apopka's St. Paul AME Church and Pastor D. Dunston, formerly of Progressive Holiness Freewill Church of Apopka, each really spoke about the issues relative to crime.

This panel was received very well with lots of enthusiasm and understanding from among the group participating. Jehovah God bestowed a blessing on that Tuesday, August 4, day by holding back the much needed rains that we are so accustomed to receiving this time of year and this allowed many encouraged citizens to attend.

According to Ms. Linda's visions for next year, in 2010, hopefully the affair will be held under a large tent in which 200 persons can be seated by blocking off portions of a street in order to accommodate a tent of that size, encouraging citizens to attend rain or shine.

Olmstead Publishing LLC

Slim, along with the citizens, wish to thank Ms. Linda Lee for her efforts and concerns for our community. "Go, Sister Girl, Go!"

Apopka woman holds many responsible positions in New York City

William and Bertha Gladden, Sr., of Apopka were an old pioneer family of Apopka during the 20th century. Their eldest daughter, Carolyn Elizabeth Gladden, was born and nurtured in Savannah, Georgia in the early 1930s and attended the local primary (Florence Street School) and secondary (Culyer Street School) educational facilities in Chatham County, completing both of those academic phases in approximately 1950.

Although reared in that area of Savannah, she constantly spent summer vacation and Christmas holidays in Apopka with her mother and father at one point in time. Carolyn's grandparents, along with her mother and father, were advocates for pursuing higher educational skills; thus insisting she enroll at Georgia State Industrial College (also known as Savannah State College) then located in Thunderbolt, Georgia. This was also the school that her father and mother attended.

Carolyn started the necessary college academic requirements for graduation, beginning in 1950 and climaxing after four years in 1954 with a bachelor's degree. While at SSC she became a charter member of the Delta Sigma Theta sorority.

Receiving a bachelor of arts degree in education, she was certified to teach in Georgia (near Brunswick) and did so for two years. She then applied in Florida for teaching certification and passed the examination and landed employment as a teacher at Hungerford High School in Eatonville for one year.

Deciding in 1958 to upgrade her academic credentials for teaching prompted her to venture to New York City to attend New York University and the Fordham University School of Social Service. She obtained a master's degree in social work and was licensed in 1968. In 1970, after further education, she was accepted into the Academy of Certified Social Workers in 1970

In the early 1960s, Carolyn was wed to Mr. Marcus McBain, who was a native of the Caribbean Islands. Carolyn McBain is a devoted member of St. Charles Borromeo Roman Catholic Church in New York City, where she is active in the Altar Rosary Society and the Bereavement Committee. Her personal ministry involves visitation and contact with the sick in her parrish.

Mrs. McBain's endeavors and experiences in the Harlem and West Tremont communities have lasted at least forty-five years. Prior to her retirement in 1996 from the New York City

Department of Education, District 75, Division of Special Education, she served thirty-two years as a New York City employee in various capacities. Her long distinguished service included working to provide foster homes for older and handicapped persons as a family services worker, a child protective service counselor and several positions at the Bronx and Borough of Manhattan Community Colleges.

Presently, Mrs. McBain is employed, as of this penning, part-time with Steinway Child and Family Services, Inc., as well as Esplanade Gardens NORC as a peer counselor. There she encourages seniors to participate in quality of life activities including tai chi, theater, opera, and health-related programs. Carolyn McBain holds active membership in numerous organizations including being a charter member and past president of the North Manhattan Alumnae Chapter of Delta Sigma Theta Sorority, Inc. and the Esplanade Gardens Building #2, past vice-president. She holds membership with the Martin Luther King, Jr. Democratic Club; National Council of Negro Women; NAACP and National Association of Social Workers.

Carolyn is the immediate past northern vice president of Savannah State University National Alumni Association; past president of the Fordham

University School of Social Service Alumni Association and a former member of the board of directors of the Upper Manhattan Empowerment Zone (2002-2006). Currently, she serves on the board of BRISC. Mrs. McBain is a member of the citywide Mental Health Coalition for Black Elderly. This group is currently seeking funds to provide educational training for personal homecare givers for the elderly. This is a primary concern and focus for Mrs. McBain–improving the quality and access to care giving for the elderly.

Carolyn McBain believes strongly that as a community we must continue to live full quality lives and to assist others. Along with these many activities, Mrs. McBain still finds time to come home to Apopka three to four times a year to lend her services to friends and acquaintances here in the Apopka area. Bits 'n' Tips column originator Mildred A. Board, godmother of Carolyn, would indeed be very elated over her goddaughter's achievements in the Big Apple, especially a person with ties from Apopka, the Indoor Foliage Capital of the World. As usual, Ms. Board would definitely comment, saying, "Sister girl, you've achieved."

Surgeon had his roots in Apopka

Modern Day Physician and Surgeon--An Apopka Lad of Our Time

Douglas "Doug" Sanders was nurtured here in Apopka in the 1970s on McQueen Road, along with his parents and two siblings.

He attended primary school at Phyllis Wheatley Elementary School, where he excelled academically as a pupil during his tenure.

The secondary phase of his education initiated at Apopka High School, where his desire and appetite for learning pyramided beyond his grade level at that point in time. While at AHS, extracurricular activities pertaining to music prompted his interest in trumpet blowing precision to the extent he was awarded a musical scholarship to enroll at the University of Florida after high school graduation.

During the last three years of high school summer vacations, Doug worked in the citrus industry at Frank Sharp's Groves, Inc., adjacent to Walt Disney World in Southwest Orange County, where the owners and top management personnel constantly encouraged him and insisted that he continue furthering his education due to his mental potentials.

Upon graduation from AHS, the aforementioned scholarship in music was granted and he was accepted for enrollment at University of Florida.

In Doug's freshman and sophomore years, his mental ability pertaining to academics exceeded to the point of excellence, prompting university curriculum counselors to convince him that he should pursue pre-med rather than a music profession.

Receiving a bachelor of science degree, he was immediately accepted and admitted into the University of Florida Medical School, completing its academic requirements in four years. Doug's medical internship was accomplished and completed here in Orange County at Orlando Regional Medical Center, specializing in trauma with the number one trauma unit in our Central Florida hospital's areas.

This experience precipitated his desire to venture into strictly the surgery arena of the medical profession. Completing medical internship, he began practicing in Polk County. Within the past four years, Doug has resided and briefly practiced his surgical skills in Duval County (Jacksonville); however, he is presently in Polk County as of this penning.

Slim personally commends physician Douglas "Doug" Sanders for his achievements and most of all his being the first individual of our heritage to become a physician nurtured in the "hood" of Apopka. Congratulations, Dr. Douglas Sanders. Also, let it be known that Doug's parents and siblings were extremely instrumental in his reaching that medical plateau.

The Apopka Chief, November 13, 2009, Page 12A

Rossie Thomas helped start farmworkers clinic

Dedicated Nurse Practitioner at Apopka Farmworker's Health Center

This unique individual of colored heritage in the person of Rossie Thomas was favorably called Ms. Rossie by many who knew her. In addition to her nursing skills, she was known for preparing and distributing a delicious bread pudding within the "Soulsville" area.

Ms. Rossie was born in approximately 1936 and nurtured in Apopka on East 18th Street near South Clarcona Road. She received her primary education only a block from her home at Apopka Colored School (now known as Phyllis Wheatley School). At that point in time, ACS consisted of one large wooden building sub-divided into four classrooms that combined two different grades one year apart within each designated area for primary education (first through eighth grades).

During the phase of primary education at ACS, Rossie was an excellent student in addition to being a superb athlete playing her favorite sport, which was basketball. This athleticism and academic excellence continued while she attended Hungerford High School, where she earned her high school diploma. Former illustrious Principal Roger Williams, then at Apopka Memorial High School, hired Rossie's father, James Thomas, as the first custodian of black heritage at AMHS.

Principal Williams encouraged Rossie and other students by insisting that students, regardless of their ethnicity, were to pursue higher educational status, and on numerous instances, financially assisted them with tuition at the institution of their choice, including Rossie. Upon graduation from Hungerford High School, she applied and was accepted at the famous and illustrious Grady School of Nursing in Atlanta, Georgia.

Rossie attended for one full term, until her mothers' ongoing illness prompted the student to return to Apopka in order to perform homecare duties and other procedures for her mother. Later on, due to her previous nursing practitioner training at Grady Nursing School, Rossie was hired by the then Florida Tuberculosis Sanitarium, south of Clarcona, as a nurse practitioner associate. The hospital eventually discontinued treating patients with the aforementioned disease; however, the existing building was converted to accommodate and treat children with special medical needs under the name Suniland Children's Hospital.

It was in this facility that Rossie remained in a supervisory nursing position. Again Principal Roger Williams came into her life through his administrative position as principal at AMHS, initiating a pilot program called Migrant Education that was in dire need of her experience. Thus, Rossie was hired as a teacher's aide for Orange County Public Schools at AMHS, where she served for several years.

A charitable Catholic organization set in motion the groundwork to establish a health center for low-income families and farm workers in the impoverished area of Apopka and nearby portions of Orange County with similar needs. They requested her services and expertise relative to health issues and referrals with an offer of permanent employment.

At that point in time, while on summer vacation, Rossie resigned her duties with OCPS and assumed the role of being the first nurse practitioner, along with a physician, for the Apopka Family Health Center, then located in a large mobile house trailer at East Eighth Street and South Central Avenue (Sanders Estate Properties). After the Sanders decided not to sell portions of the then-occupied land, so the center could construct adequate medical facilities and expand to accommodate the ever growing populous, the organization eventually negotiated to purchase land where the present day site is nowadays on South Forest Avenue and East Seventh Street, just slightly east of the Midland Railroad tracks.

The demands at the Apopka Center for Healthcare pyramided to the extent that it required expansion of its existing medical facilities plus professional staffing of nurses and physicians. In order to benefit the agriculture industries' volume of patients in dire need of medical treatment from the surrounding areas of Northwest and Southwest Orange County, numerous citrus and vegetable growers became involved administratively and financially. They established a clinic at Harlem Heights Labor Camp located on South SR 545 near the Old Turkey Farm and Ms. Rossie and a physician commuted from Apopka twice per week to medically treat or advise patients, usually on a walk-in basis.

The Harlem Heights area, being off normal transportation routes, encouraged the organization to lease a building in Winter Garden from Roper Citrus Growers west of Dillard Street and slightly south of West Plant Street and convert it into an up-scale medical facility. At that point in time, it became accessible for patients in southwest Orange and Lake counties that Ms. Rossie worked with occasionally.

Over the years of her employment, she performed in all phases of nursing available at the centers, especially instilling in patients the need for consistent healthcare and necessary referrals not provided at the center. Prior to retirement, Ms. Rossie received one of the few awards given for Distinguished Employee for her dedicated services. The governing board, after her term as an employee, unanimously requested her to become a governing board member. Let it be noted Ms. Rossie was the first in the field of nursing practitioner to assist in establishing and organizing the health center facilities, as we know them nowadays. Slim along with many patients thank Ms. Rossie for her dedication, care, concern, understanding and sincere compassion.

Labor Day was a day of work for some people

Past Labor Day Festivals at Edgewood Cemetery

Labor is a human effort either physical or mental or both, directed to some useful and productive end. Although labor parties began to flourish in the late 19th century, it was some years later that the first Monday of September of every year was considered Labor Day, a legal American holiday.

During the 1940s through the 1950s, persons of Apopka's ghetto area annually celebrated Labor Day at Edgewood Cemetery by performing landscaping labor.

The Colored Cemetery portion of Greenwood-Edgewood Cemetery in Apopka has been known since the late 19th century into the 20th century as traditionally where persons of color were only buried. Shortly after the mid-20th century, the area's name changed along with the policy in reference to burial, regardless of ethnicity.

Stemming from population expansion and the deplorable unkempt vegetation growth for years at the Colored Cemetery during the 1940s, Negro entrepreneurs of Apopka, along with several concerned citizens of similar ethnicity, below TO&A Railroad established an organization assuming the stewardship for plot sales and maintenance. It was known as the Apopka Colored Cemetery Association, consisting of the overseer's board that included Martha A. Board, Tom Barnes, Arthur Willis, Allen Chisholm, Bill Chandler, Richard and Maggie Hayward, Hannah Williams and M. Gladden.

The idea of the festival came from a lack of financial attributes generated from plot sales or massive donations. Therefore, it was deemed necessary to have the "blackbelt" community participants and family members of the deceased to allot time and effort once per year relative to addressing the landscaping issues.

To enhance this landscaping project, each proprietor of the Apopka ghetto area contributed financially for fish, bread, lemonade, cooking utensils, cooking ingredients, transportation and, to some extent, necessary landscaping tools. Several years beyond the 20th century halfway mark, the Apopka Colored Cemetery Association unanimously concurred to let the City of Apopka own the cemetery by transferring of deeds, sell plots whenever requested and be responsible for complete landscaping when needed. That's how we celebrated Labor Day in the 1940s into the 1950s (smile).

23 Apopka Colored Cemetery Association gave the cemetery to the City of Apopka. Photo Dr.O, 2015.

Few blacks could attend high school during the late 1800s to early 1900s

Struggling For Education Beyond Eight Grades--Legislation brought changes to Orange County Public Schools in Rural Areas

Within Orange County, certain northwest rural areas consisted of a small Negro population starting in the late 19th century into the 20th century (1947).

Education for Negroes remained at the primary level only, offering pupils the equivalent of an eighth grade education, due to the fact there was only one public high school (Jones High) in the entire Orange County Public School system, at that point in time, for persons of color to complete secondary education.

Once students of this ethnicity reached that plateau of primary education (eighth grade), the majority of families could not financially afford commuters fees nor board their student in Orlando. There was one black private high school (Hungerford) in Orange County; however, it strictly required from parents all financial support for student's board, room and tuition fees for the final four years of secondary education.

If by some ways and means a student was awarded a financial supported scholarship, this was acceptable at Hungerford.

Of those pupils of the aforementioned heritage residing in those rural OCPS areas that completed the primary phase of education, 99 percent of them were immediately thrust into the workforce, doing common labor. Finally, through legislation, it was absolutely necessary to adopt, pass and enforce the children's labor laws, so students of those rural areas were not forced into labor situations because OCPS did not have secondary education facilities for pupils.

Hungerford High School in Eatonville, a private institution for pupils of Negro heritage, negotiated an educational agreement in 1947 with OCPS to accept public school students of colored heritage from the Northwest sections of Orange County, in addition to Maitland, Forest City and Winter Park, thus alleviating numerous issues pertaining to integration, school bus transportation, building new high school facilities and continuation of education beyond the eighth grade.

In addition, OCPS administrative officials would develop and be responsible for a school bus transportation system, beginning in approximately 1947, for pupils of color in the rural areas of

Northwest Orange County to Hungerford High School.

After 10 years with an agreement between OCPS and Hungerford, the Northwest Orange County was granted authority to construct and make operational a high school facility for persons of color within that rural sector (Apopka) to accommodate pupils from Clarcona, Lake Apopka, Plymouth, Zellwood, Fuller's Crossing, and Tangerine.

Integration arrived some 22 years (1969) later. In conclusion, just for a moment, all present-day students of any ethnicity or area heretofore mentioned should think about the struggles and sacrifices made to ascertain a primary and secondary education for you by your parents and grandparents. It should not warrant you milling under stately looking oak trees, standing on street corners and storefronts, providing illicit pharmaceutical products for sale, use and abuse, or committing robbery and prostitution.

Henry Glover was the first black policeman

"Chief" Henry Glover--First Policeman of Negro Heritage in Apopka

In this penning, Slim will brief the reader on events or incidents that occurred that precipitated the City of Apopka to employ Henry Glover as a policeman during the 1940s. Negro policemen or patrolmen with the authority of a certified law enforcement officer to submit charges alleged or arrest any ethnicity were very rare in Florida, until the WWII era (1943-1945).

At this point in the 1940s, the ways of life in Apopka's small area changed drastically. Edwards Field was converted into a U.S. Army base to house soldiers (whites and Negroes). [WWII German prisoners, who were primarily utilized in agriculture endeavors, were transported from a base detention center in Leesburg for labor.]

Also, the two major railway corporations (SAL Railroad and ACL Railroad) were continuing their massive repairs and building of new tracks to accommodate the war efforts and expansion of needed business facilities.

Olmstead Publishing LLC

The railroad workers who maintain the tracks then were known as the "Extra Gang," which was 99.9 percent Negro heritage.

24 James McGraw was one of Apopka's first black police officers--L>R-James 'Mitch' Carter, ?, John Holloway, Glenn Woodard, Kenneth Eldredge, Hank Carlson, James McGraw-15 Sep 1966. Entire force. AHS.

The railroad companies housed these workers within "railroad cars," usually that had the conveniences of sleeping quarters, complete hygiene facilities, galley, laundry, commissary, electricity, first aid station, steam for heating or cooking, equipment storage area and repair shop on convenient sidetracks that had an ample water supply from a municipal township nearest their designated work area.

The TO&A's (also known as the Seaboard Airline Railroad) work area was made up of Plymouth, Apopka, Lakeville, and Lockhart while the ACL work area then initiated in a Clarcona railroad section yard and included Ocoee, Fuller's Crossing, and the Clarcona-Apopka crossover. At this point in time, Apopka Police Chief Fred Risener had the responsibility of maintaining law and order with a minimum quota of law enforcement officers under his command; therefore, due to the mass invasion of workers and covering additional territory, it became necessary to employ additional much-needed police officers.

At this point, it was brought to the attention of the city fathers of Apopka, for the sake of social and safety precautions within the "ghettos," that they hire Henry Glover to be the first colored Apopka police officer to enforce law and order below the TO&A Railroad tracks.

Immediately after being hired, Henry Glover, on numerous occasions, had to administer his police authority in outlying areas of Northwest and Southwest Orange County, other than the Apopka.

This enormous task of controlling activities in the city of Apopka and outlying districts acted as a catalyst in the employment of Norman Betts of Negro heritage as a police officer to assist Henry

Glover as they patrolled in a 1935 Ford two-door six days per week. These two police officers provided an access to public safety and social issues during their entire tenure until the late 1940s. After the 1940s era, the City of Apopka did not employ police officers of Negro heritage until the early 1960s when James McGrath from Alabama was hired.

25 Edwards Field-'Apopka Boys' returned WWII. Back: William Bogar, Elwood Ustler, Bruce Stephens, Justin Lovell. Middle: Jack Hall, ?, Riley Byrd Gilbert, Joel Reid?, Leslie Grantham? Front: John H. Land, Furman Driggers, Forrest Conway, Garrett Gilliam. Photo from Land family.

Apopka woman excels in criminal justice field

Juvenile Justice Officer

Dr. Monica Webb was an extraordinary and unique individual in the zenith of her profession as a supervisor for the Florida juvenile justice system pertaining to disciplinary measures and punishment. She was raised in Apopka, along with four siblings, shortly after the mid-20th century by their parents, Willie "Coach" Webb and Polly Webb.

Monica's primary education phase was completed at Phyllis Wheatley Elementary School. Secondary education, at that point in time, was offered at Apopka High School, under the watchful eyes of the illustrious principal Roger Williams, for students of Northwest Orange County. Monica was far above the average grade point during her four-year tenure prior to graduation.

She was readily accepted for admission at Florida State University in Tallahassee, where she obtained a bachelor of science degree in criminal justice. Since receiving her BS, she has hopes of earning a master's degree followed by Ph.D. in the related field in the very near future.

Upon completing the required academic program at FSU, she was immediately employed by the Florida Department of Juvenile Justice here in Orange County. Throughout numerous years since being employed at FDJJ, her constant studying, experience and dedication has put Monica into the status of being named the number one supervisor in that category of juvenile justice for the entire state, when state officials recently honored her in 2006.

Nowadays, she travels throughout Florida, advising and assisting newcomers within the FDJJ. It has been Slim's observation, on many occasions, especially in Northwest Orange County, that she puts forth effort, time, and concern to the resolution of juvenile problems on a one-on-one basis, even when not requested by parties involved.

The majority of citizens in the Apopka area (project, hood, slums, Soulsville, blackbelt, ghetto) respect her honesty and concrete positive information pertaining to juvenile issues and her ability to expedite existing problems. Monica! Slim reflects on a time when you were a child growing up within our neighborhood only three doors from each other and how you always, as a child and young adult, projected wanting to achieve something positive to substantiate your place in society in a way that's beneficial to mankind.

Thanks for your efforts and expertise to avert so many youngsters from going astray or being a burden on society. Kids, whether good or bad, will be society's leaders of tomorrow (smile).

Regardless of how insignificant it might appear, Monica, you've definitely made a difference among numerous juveniles and their families. Hopefully, that petite percentage of youngsters who have been willing to adhere to the tenets of society and the ten commandments shall carry us through many forms of wanted attributes that we need to see in society. Again, Slim and many others thank you very much, Ms. Monica Webb.

Time	Event
24000	Paleo-Indians Marion County
5300	BC Windover Pond, Titusville
2000	BC Fired Pottery in Florida
1450	BC Oldest shell midden (burial mound) in the East--Horr's Island
500	BC Spread of people across the peninsula
0	
500	
1000	
1100	Timucuan Indians—Jacksonville Dig site
1200	
1300	
1400	
1500	@ 350,000 inhabitants of peninsula 1513 Ponce de Leon lands near Canaveral—Spanish Rule Begins
1600	
1700	Entry of Seminole people 1763 British Rule Begins 1783 Spanish Rule Begins By 1800 Many indigenous tribes extinct
1800	1822 U.S. Florida Territorial Period Begins—Gov. A. Jackson Area known as Saint Johns County 1824 Area below St Johns River renamed Mosquito County 1845 State of Florida Established, Area renamed Orange County 1882 City of Apopka Established
1900	
2000	

26 Some Events of the Peninsula Land Mass Known as Florida. DrO.

The Apopka Chief, December 25, 2009, Page 11A

Agriculture brought many people to Apopka

Influential Persons of Northwest Orange County (1849-1949)

The history and growth of Apopka and Zellwood reminded Slim as to how twin cities in this good old USA managed themselves in their infancy to promote their present day achievements. The beginnings of these two cities of Apopka and Zellwood came about in the mid-19th century with similar means and visions for their startups.

The proximity to the waterways and railroads precipitated a more rapid growth for Apopka versus Zellwood. Wekiva River and Clay Springs were navigable waterways near Apopka and there were two railroad companies (Jacksonville, Tampa & Key West Railroad; Orange Belt Railroad).

Lake Apopka, being nearer to Zellwood, was the headwaters of the chain of lakes into the Ocklawaha River that led into the St. Johns River near Palatka; however, very few families utilized this method of navigable waterways into Zellwood due to most vessels' draft.

The TO&A Railroad did not go into Zellwood until the 1880s; therefore, very few people ventured into the Zellwood area because of the lack

Olmstead Publishing LLC

of traditional means of travel. There were numerous men and women that were extremely instrumental in this process – E. J. Ryan, Amos D. Starbird and sons, J. L. Giles, Sarah Mead, John Tunno Champneys, Mrs. Alfred Eldredge, T. Elwood Zell, J. G. Grossenbacher, W. R. McLeod, Ella Walls, William A. Lovell, James R. Stewart, George Oden, Thomas C. Buchan, Mattie M. Spicker, J. D. Mitchell, Minnie Vick, Bennett Land Sr., Harry Ustler, William C. Goolsby, Ella McGee, H. K. Fuller, Luther F. Tilden, W. G. Talton, William S. Delk, William Braxton, and Bragg Hammond.

27 Stone from a gristmill operated by Judge W. A. Mills and son Columbus at Mill Creek, now in Wekiwa Springs State Park. 1860-1870s. Donated by John H. Land, see at the Museum of the Apopkans, 5th Steet. Photo by DrO 2014.

Due to the gigantic number of names needing noting, please accept Slim's apology for omitting any more names. Several other individuals to appear in this penning also played a very significant role. However, the aforementioned pioneers were also significant in the development of Northwest Orange County, beginning in approximately 1875 and continuing well into the 1940s.

James L. Giles was an attorney in the area and once mayor of Orlando during this early period in and around 1850-1880. In approximately the 1870s, Richard Goldsborough Robinson arrived in the Apopka-Zellwood area, along with a petite group of early pioneers, including Luther F. Tilden, S. M. Pike, J. S. Womble, T. A. Vick, H. K. Fuller, T. Elwood Zell and a few more not intentionally omitted.

R. G. Robinson was quite instrumental in being a booster for the area's growth and economical probability. In and around the latter 1870s, his business endeavors included clearing, planting, and citrus grove management for absentee owners. Ms. Anna M. L. Earle, an absentee citrus grove owner that R. G. worked for, stipulated in her will after expenses the proceeds were to be distributed to a Philadelphia hospital, Episcopal mission in Zellwood and a children's home in Maryland.

In the 1880s, the St. James Mission was created in the earlier days of Zellwood, where R. G. Robinson was a lay reader until 1885. R. G. Robinson served as a Florida legislator from 1885 until 1889. During this period, Osceola County did not exist, and the area was considered a portion of Orange County and Lake County. Citizens of that vast area wanted better representation at the state level; therefore, they initiated action to establish a new county seat of the aforementioned vast area.

R. G. Robinson spearheaded that struggle through numerous legislations and was successful in creating a boundary line to establish the new county of Osceola as we know it today and compromising with Lake County to let Zellwood and Tangerine remain part of Orange County, which was agreeable to all parties. R.G. Robinson continued residing in Zellwood for periods of time, also serving as Justice of the Peace.

In 1894-1895, he was on a committee promoting an exhibit at the Atlanta Cotton States. T. Elwood Zell, for whom Zellwood is named, arrived from Pennsylvania after the Civil War. In approximately 1875, he recruited many notable families and entrepreneurs by promoting the area as a place for winter residency and citrus production.

The Apopka Chief, January 1, 2010, Page 9A

Early settlers planted citrus

Influential Persons of Northwest Orange County (1849-1949)

In the 1880s, Dr. C. H. Lampheon and Dr. M. G. McDonald were serving as physicians for Plymouth and Zellwood. Richard Whitney resided in Zellwood in the late 1890s, after being enticed by Florida's superb enjoyable winter weather and several business ventures. During the 1920s-1930s, Whitney was president of the New York Stock Exchange for five terms. Whitney purchased stock in the State Bank of Apopka in 1930, thus becoming the majority stockholder and vice president during the financial crisis of the 1930s. He also owned 30,000 acres of hunting preserves in Northwest Orange County.

In approximately 1939, Whitney immediately disposed of his stock at the State Bank of Apopka and resigned as vice president after being charged with embezzlement resulting from his business in New York. He wanted to eliminate the thought that the Apopka bank might be associated with his existing charges. After serving his incarceration time at Sing Sing, Whitney returned to Florida and tried his hand at numerous business ventures while living in Mt. Plymouth for many years into the 1940s.

William Edwards was another early developer along with several other notable individuals, including John T. Pirie, James Laughlin, and J. G. Grossenbacher. "Old man" Charlie Grinnell who, at the time of this writing, is approaching the century mark. Slim was privileged to meet him, and he spoke of the growth of the area and countless achievements of the early pioneers of that era in Apopka and Zellwood's development.

William Edwards, affiliated with numerous organizations (YMCA and Moody Evangelistic Crusade), was Scottish-born and ventured into Chicago in the late 19th century. Once in the Apopka and Zellwood area in the 19th and 20th century, he was a highly regarded, important driving force pertaining to estate management. He was responsible for recruiting families for area entrepreneurships, citrus endeavors, cattle breeding, and banking.

According to recorded history, he was noted as being the best of the best during that era. Prior to coming to Florida, while he was still in Chicago, his expertise in management skills was noticed by John T. Pirie of Lake Forest, Illinois, president and board chairman of a prestige Chicago dry good firm. John

T., without reservation, hired Edwards to manage Pirie's estate (Errol Farm) in Northwest Orange County.

In addition to managing Pirie's Estate, he also managed the estate of James Laughlin, a steel magnate from Pennsylvania, this being one of the many famous estates of Zellwood. Edwards faithfully served on the Orange County branch of President Herbert Hoover's Food Administration. He also served long terms on the Orange County School Board for district three. William Edwards also was president of Plymouth Citrus Growers Exchange for 20 years.

Edwards was instrumental in establishing the State Bank of Apopka in 1912 due to his persistence and networking colleagues in the financial arena. In 1921, Edwards, while at PCGE, had an electricity-generating plant installed that was capable of supplying electricity for Plymouth and Zellwood when their lifestyle mandated 24-hour electricity. The Apopka baseball stadium was named in his honor and the State Bank of Apopka honored him for the contributions and efforts he gave so willingly to Apopka and Zellwood. William Edwards without a doubt left a legacy to behold in our Northwest Orange County.

In and around 1904, James W. "Sawgrass" Jones, who was from Tennessee and living in Texas temporarily, became one of Zellwood's big boosters due to its muck lands' potential for producing vegetable crops at a rapid pace more than once per year. Sawgrass had difficulties initially with drainage and dehydration that caused him to abandon the project until 1910, when an engineering scientist resolved the uncontrollable water levels.

Professor E. W. Fly, around 1914, was a teacher in management at Apopka High School. In 1924, along with several of the Zellwood Methodists, he began constructing a new church by negotiating a loan from Orange County Building and Loan Association. E. W. Fly, in the 1920s, became one of Plymouth Citrus Growers Exchange's leading board members and, in 1935, he became president of PCGE. During WWII, Apopka, Plymouth and Zellwood had a vehicular tire rationing board consisting of John Ustler, R. T. Carlton and E. W. Fly.

When the State Bank of Apopka was sold in 1947 to R. T. Carlton & Associates, E. W. Fly became a board member. He was an integral part of the growth of Apopka and in the move to recruit families into the areas of Apopka and Zellwood through his connections with the banking industry.

Jules Vann, sometime referred as Jules Vance, of Negro ethnicity was born in North Carolina in 1870 and ventured into the Zellwood area at the age of 59 around the 1930s. He became well known and prosperous in farming traditions, including citrus growing and acquiring numerous parcels of property southward between U.S. Highway 441 and the TO&A Railroad present day railroad tracks in Zellwood. At one point in time, it was noted he operated a mom and pop type of store near U.S. Highway 441 in the area. It is mentioned by several of the old timers that Vann donated a small portion of land for Zellwood Colored School (also known as Fredrick Douglas Elementary) during that era. The vision and the foresight of all these individuals and many others led to the positive sizeable growth financially, economically and physically of these twin cities.

28 John T. Pirie's estate in Plymouth area, now known as Errol Estate. Photo AHS.

The Apopka Chief, January 8, 2010, Page 10A

Apopka man had long career in Miami

Country Boy Policeman in Miami

L. G. Nolle was a young man who was nurtured here in Apopka and resided at Northwest Second Street and North Central Avenue, along with his siblings and mother, Mrs. Lillian Nolle, during the 1920-1930s near Amos D. Starbird's elegant home site.

Slim, during the course of this penning, will refer to L.G. Nolle as "Captain." Prior to venturing into Miami to seek law enforcement employment many years before the halfway mark of the 20th century, Captain had the opportunity to witness, on numerous occasions, the procedures of several competent law enforcement officers in Apopka; namely, H. D. Miley, Fred Risener and J. S. Parrish.

This proved to be beneficial prior to his tenure with the Miami Police Department in the late 1930s. Captain, when employed by the Miami Police Department, was a policeman when that department's policy was that employment was strictly for officers of white ethnicity only. However, he had previous experiences in law enforcement that enhanced Nolle's advantages in the field relative to the race card.

At that point in time, the City of Miami did not have Negroes as police officers in any capacity until the late 1940s, and then they were called patrolmen without the authority or powers of a certified police officer.

By this time, Captain had risen in rank, and in the 1950s, he was assigned as commanding officer of a special 11th Street Precinct (booking office, jail and courtrooms) composed of all Negro judges, patrolmen and correction officers recently hired by the city on a first time trial basis. At this point in time, black patrolmen were designated as police officers like their white counterparts, with the same authority pertaining to charges or arresting.

Although Captain's ethnicity was totally different from personnel under his command, his past experiences gained in Apopka increased his notoriety, thus enhancing his ability to deal with another race and their issues, and assuring him an excellent rapport in race relations during his entire tenure as an officer of the Miami Police Department assigned to a predominately Negro area precinct as commander.

At one point in time, he supervised approximately 50 police officers, 12 correction officers, the jail facilities at the precinct and jail trustees, all, as previously mentioned, of Negro heritage. In 1957, Slim was in Miami and had the privilege of meeting Captain, and we reflected upon our knowledge of Apopka, its pioneer citizens and our immediate families, with whom we both were acquainted. We quite often drove from Miami to Apopka together for visits during 1957-1960. Slim, along with many citizens of that era, really appreciated his unique understanding of race relations at that point in time. Thanks, Captain!

29 Nolle House built 1900 at 22 South Central Avenue. Photo AHS.

The Apopka Chief, January 15, 2010, Page 10A

'Garbage men' make a great contribution to Apopka society

Sanitation Engineers--Collection and Maintenance of Waste Keeps Area Clean

The average person has little regards for what society literally calls the neighborhood "garbage man." Most citizens have the tendency to look down upon that form of endeavor in a degrading manner; therefore the profession is placed within the lower standards of livelihood in most sectors of this good old U.S.A.

Often Slim recalls, while living in New York City during the latter 1960s, the garbage men, firemen and policemen were all on the same identical pay scale ($30,000 per annum plus health insurance, retirement benefits, vacation pay and overtime pay), placing them, at that point in time, with the highest-paid NYC employees in most categories of employment.

Most citizens in NYC considered the garbage man position, relative to salary regardless of the type of tasks it entailed, to be a highly respected profession. Once an area's population starts growing, it becomes a necessity for its society to maintain garbage men to perform their jobs to

Olmstead Publishing LLC

control pollution, littering, diseases, methods of disposal and potential energy sources.

This penning stems from Slim's observation of the garbage and waste materials over periods of numerous years within city and county areas. Slim recalls, while living in the Reedy Creek District of Orange County in the 1980s, the Orange County commissioners unanimously approved initiating garbage and trash collection throughout its county by employing a waste management firm. When households or businesses were totally responsible for disposing of their trash, some of those patrons placed refuse on roadways, vacant lots, open pits (clay, sand, rock), buried waste at random, or constantly stored refuse on their premises.

Since 1989 in Apopka, several waste management firms have bid and contracted to render this service to eliminate the above issues; therefore, they should be commended for their performances and concerns. As of this penning, Slim makes reference to one person employed by a waste management company in the Apopka area. Mario Bridges was a young man who was considered by all patrons in the area as being the best garbage man over a two-year period in regards to how he handles waste products with such professionalism and concern for the entire neighborhood, not overlooking garbage can pickups at that moment and spillage.

Thanks, Mario! The patrons of this area really appreciate your personal efforts and concerns for the community. Keep it clean, soul brother! (smile)

The Apopka Chief, January 22, 2010, Page 14A

Teacher was a big influence on all areas of life in Apopka

James Davis of Apopka--Versatile Teacher

Although this professor is slightly agewise ahead of me, I am indeed well acquainted with and involved in many of his upbringing years, hardships and achievements.

30 **Walter A. Davis, Sr., Father, Born May 3, 1880, Died Oct 23, 1963, Intered in Edgewood Cemetery.** Photo by DrO 2015

James Davis, of Negro heritage, was born during the 1920 depression years and nurtured in Orange County. His father, Walter A. Davis, at that point in time, owned 20 acres approximately one-fourth of a mile east of the Midland Railroad tracks as it crosses East Cleveland Street in a north-south direction in Apopka originating from Clarcona.

James Davis's primary education initiated at Apopka Colored School, which was a large wooden building divided into four separate classrooms that held two grades (one grade above the other) taught by one teacher for the entire school term year. At that time, the school was located at 18th Street and Lake Avenue, thus being almost one-and-one-half miles walking distance from his home.

Public school secondary education in Orange County for a person of Davis's heritage, at that point in time, was only available at Jones High School in Orlando, so he decided to attend under very unusual circumstances.

While enrolled at Jones, he became very familiar with the powers to be, regular people and conditions in the Orlando-Apopka area.

Years later, this knowledge was an immeasurable asset to his teaching profession, political, business and social involvement in the entire Orange County area. Most young men in the early 1940s were drafted or volunteered for military duty obligations, placing Davis as a candidate with Uncle Sam's military service for a tour of duty. Sometime in the 1940s, while employed by former Orange County Commissioner

John Talton in his citrus groves, he sustained an injury to his ankle-leg area that precipitated a tremendous change in his future endeavors and achievements.

James decided to utilize his Veteran's Administration benefits to pursue further education at then Florida A&M College, earning a bachelor's degree that immediately thrust him into a teaching profession with Orange County Public Schools (Jones High) in the latter 1950s.

At this point in time, James Davis became the first person of his heritage in Orange County to be certified as a licensed master electrician, allowing him to teach and install electricity anywhere in Florida. In the 1950s, James Davis, after numerous encounters with the illustrious Sheriff Dave Starr for Orange County, became quite influential in getting Sheriff Starr to hire deputies of Negro heritage with the authority to bring charges or arrest offenders when laws were broken by any person or group, regardless of their ethnicity.

That moment of hiring deputies of non-white ethnicity became famous among law enforcement agencies in the tri-counties area by establishing Car 44 (Demps-Crooms), that even today, still remains as a part of the history of that era.

In the latter 1950s, John T. Vereen of Negro heritage had achieved extensive notoriety in the citrus industry with which James Davis was well acquainted and experienced. This precipitated Davis to form a corporation with Vereen.

James met and married Loretha Quartman, a talented singer and music teacher for OCPS, who was a niece of a prominent physician, Dr. Wells of Negro heritage of Orlando. Z. L. Riley, a longtime resident, and renowned, competent tailor of the Orlando area, was president and spokesperson of the Orlando Negro Chamber of Commerce for numerous years. James Davis was later voted by the citizens to replace the incumbent Riley as president.

Upon inheriting the leadership, it was agreed to discontinue "Negro" from its title. After several years of teaching industrial arts for OCPS, he was assigned to become principal at his hometown school, Apopka Colored School, during the summer of 1966, a job he turned down for positions for the state of Floridain Tallahassee, where he served in several administrative positions.

Later James Davis was appointed at his college alma mater, as the president's assistant in several capacities, one being a lobbyist, for the next 35 years until retiring recently. James Davis was Slim's employer at one point in time, and they had multiple conversations about Davis assisting students to obtain grants, tutoring, dormitory accommodations, off-campus room and board, student-athlete programs, employment after graduation, special assistance for students from Central Florida, and jobs in and around college area. A million thanks from all of us.

Entrepreneurs built up Apopka

Henry Terrell, a Negro born and educated in the 1880s in Florida migrated into Tangerine from Zellwood at the climax of the 19th century, pursuing his trade as a competent and renowned blacksmith. Although this period of time involved the transition from the horse and buggy days to automotive innovations, his endeavors were still needed and well-received throughout Lake, Seminole and Orange counties well into the 1940s.

Mules, horses, cultivation equipment, harnesses and wagons were much in demand for various forms of restoration, roadwork, transportation, farming and recreation purposes. During his tenure, Henry Terrell acquired numerous parcels of property in Tangerine; also he established a "mom and pop" store for his ethnic neighborhood. Presently, the old mom and pop store building still exists. Henry Terrell was extremely interested in sandlot baseball for Negroes in the Tri-County district during that 1930-1940 era in which he managed, promoted and financially supported a baseball team in Apopka. Currently, there is a roadway named Terrell Road in his honor for contributions he gave so willingly within the Tangerine Negro community.

Herman "H. M." Mobley, who was born in Georgia in approximately 1870, was another entrepreneur of Negro heritage and considered one of the early pioneer persons of his ethnicity. He migrated from Georgia into Northwest Orange County, engaging in grocery store endeavors as a source of livelihood. His business initiated in the Zellwood area known as the Coen Groves Quarters (nowadays, an upscale community called Zellwood Station) in the early 1900s.

Later, in the second decade of the 1900s, Mr. H. M. Mobley ventured into Apopka, establishing a general grocery store on South Central Avenue near the TO&A Railroad tracks; however, that facility was destroyed along with many other Apopka buildings during a period of devastating storms. H. M. Mobley immediately relocated on East Ninth Street between South Central Avenue and South Park Avenue, thus having a supported business in the neighborhood well into the 1950s, and for a brief period, even after his demise.

On South Park Avenue, between 11th Street (aka Bishop G. H. Washington Street) and 12th Street in Apopka, an entrepreneur of color, namely Mrs. Ella Walls, born in 1873 in Pennsylvania, constructed numerous shanty shotgun houses from the surplus lumber, then called "slabs," that were free just for the asking at the Consumers Lumber & Veneer Company mill in Apopka. Once they were built, Mrs. Walls rented to families seeking a residency. The majority of those shotgun-type shanty houses existed well into 1960s.

31 Shotgun shanty house at 34 W 13th St (built 1940). Photo Dr. O. 2015 02

On the southeast corner of South Central Avenue at 12th Street in Apopka remains the home of entrepreneur Mrs. Mary Henry. It was built in the early portion of the 20th century and is still intact and occupied. Mrs. Henry constructed shotgun shanty houses from surplus "slabs" materials like her competitor, Mrs. Ella Walls, who was located just around the corner on South Park Avenue.

She rented those crudely constructed shanty shotgun houses within the two small citrus groves on her property. The rental period of these shanty shotgun houses initiated in the 1910s and continued into the 1960s, even after her demise. Although Mrs. Henry's religious affiliation was Methodist, a church was built in the 1980s on one of her citrus grove properties after her heirs sold the property. It currently is a thriving church called The Lighthouse under the leadership of Bishop Ronnie Davis of Apopka and Brooklyn, N.Y.

Former City of Apopka Commissioner Alonzo Williams Jr., elected consecutively over a period of 20 years by popular vote beginning in the 1970s, was the first of his race in Apopka to attain that status. His fraternal grandmother Epsie Williams, a renowned, competent midwife who resided in Clarcona in the 1920s, utilized her God-given skills as a midwife for both races in the immediate area, even after moving to Apopka in the 1950s. Prior to that point in time, Dr. Thomas E. McBride, famous competent, renowned physician, especially in Northwest Orange County, also sanctioned Mrs. Epsie Williams in the birthing profession, regardless of ethnicity.

The Apopka Chief, February 19, 2010, Page 14A

Real Estate agent offered low payment plans for property

Mrs. Rosa Barnes, a Negro, was a competent and renowned midwife in the immediate areas of Orange, Lake and Seminole counties during the early 20th century. Mrs. Barnes was nurtured in the Clarcona area at her family estate near the Wallace-Richardson private airfield that, even today, is used for active service if needed. Mrs. Barnes assisted the average mother professionally during labor at this point in time, sanctioned by Dr. T. E. "Tommy" McBride, who delegated 99 percent of birthing assistance to Rosa. Most babies born during the 1900s to 1950s were assisted by Rosa Barnes, Epise Williams and Mrs. Pickett, who were the midwives for persons of color.

L. T. Hunt, a licensed real estate entrepreneur not of Slim's ethnicity, resided in Longwood, but spent 99 percent of his time and efforts in Apopka, transacting real estate and housing negotiations within the "ghetto." He should be recognized as being very instrumental in Negroes acquiring property and homes in the early 20th century in Apopka, especially below the TO&A Railroad tracks (SAL) and west of the Midland Railroad tracks (ACL). Most persons in the 1930s-1950s of Slim's race could not afford property or homes; nevertheless, Hunt would offer low interest rates along with a low payment plan on property or constructing a home to the potential buyer over a period of eight years or less. Slim recalls some payment plans being $2.50 per week until the balance was paid off (smile).

Believe me, seldom did foreclosures occur as they do nowadays. L. T. Hunt's "calling card" at that period was his black 1929 Model A Ford coupe with a tire rack attached to the rumble seat, thus being extremely noticeable as he transacted business. In conclusion, it stands to reason why so many individuals of color in Apopka negotiating with L. T. Hunt in acquiring property or homes were successful. Thanks to Slim's persons of color and L. T. Hunt for their superb vision.

There were numerous educators initiating in the 1920s-1950s who should be noted: Claudia Sims, Ella J. Sanders, Alean Gladden, Martha A. Board, Sally Cason, Marie S. Gladden, Booker T. Reddick, Emma W. Walls, Verdie Hooper, C. W. Jennings, S. F. "Shag" Harris, Edith H. Williams, Bertha B. Gladden, Levy Gregg, Mildred A. Board and Leroy Brown. Slim and many students taught by these educators do indeed thank you all for your efforts, patience, time, finances and the occasionally corporal punishments (smile).

The City of Apopka had issues collecting delinquent taxes from all ethnic property owners. On July 12, 1937, the council adopted an ordinance to segregate areas of residencies and businesses, creating a boundary utilizing the TO&A Railroad tracks as a north-south boundary marker. Whites were above and blacks were below railroad tracks so the two races would be completely separated, whether they were compliant in paying delinquent taxes or not, thus forcing persons of color to move.

Most Negro families, with the exception of Chisholm, Pickett, Logan, Flakes and Richardson, had ventured below the proposed ordinance boundary and established a neighborhood permanently below the railroad tracks. Several Negro property owners, namely Morris Chisholm, Sr., and especially those of his heritage above the TO&A Railroad tracks in the nearby "Mead's Bottom" area, objected. Chisholm, acted as spokesman for the remaining Negro families along with an influential white businessman, resident of the then mixed neighborhood. After numerous encounters with the City Council of Apopka, he was able to convince members that he and the remaining families of his ethnicity should be allowed to stay and maintain their properties. The citizens who were behind on their taxes would comply if given ample time to pay their delinquent taxes without retribution.

That ordinance was not fully enforced pertaining to the particulars for 30 years. During February 1968, that ordinance or any portion relative to said ordinance was repealed. At this point in time, between the adoption of the ordinance and repeal, the remaining Negro families, with the exception of the Chisholms, had already relinquished their properties. The Chisholm family remained until the property sold in the 1990s.

The Apopka Chief, February 26, 2010, Page 13A

More black history to come in 2011

John T. Vereen of soul brother's heritage was nurtured in Orange and Seminole counties (Forest City) and is now retired in Plymouth at his home and citrus fruit processing area. John attended public schools locally, colleges in Florida and New York during the 1940s-1950s. Later in the 1950s, John became interested in citrus processing, initiating with the harvesting phase. During the 1960s, Vereen was publicized in several magazines as being the first person of his race to have accomplished so much in the processing arena pertaining to citrus. John harvested more citrus than his competitors (of his heritage) and had a thriving citrus juice business called "John-John" that lasted well into the 1990s. Also, John established a packinghouse processing plant that was located south of the current U.S. Highway 441 and Maitland Boulevard that was totally destroyed by fire. Nowadays, it's very interesting to chat with John as to the changes involved in citrus processing.

Francina Boykin, nurtured in Apopka, received primary and secondary education in Apopka and went on to receive a college degree. Ms. Boykin always had the desire to delve into legal and civic matters. It is without a doubt she's strictly a civic-minded individual, beginning with the civil rights issues of the 20th century. Although relatively young, she has played a significant role in arbitration for people of her heritage in areas pertaining to civil rights, public health, neighborhood watch programs, supervised sporting events at parks, public education, street maintenance, low-income housing accommodations, school zoning, and gang activities. Francina Boykin has penned numerous articles in several leading Central Florida and Jacksonville newspapers in recent years.

Nowadays, Ms. Boykin is constantly stopping at street corners for great lengths of time, conversing with youngsters about achievements, truancy, self-esteem, respect for others, dress code (boys with breeches below their buttocks; girls with too much body exposure) and offering concrete advice. Ms. Boykin has gained an outstanding level of respect and notoriety in the ghetto, and even in the up-scale communities in Orange County for her high quality of standards and the need to assist others over the years of being the "people's advocate." Francina attributes her success to the likes of the illustrious principal of Apopka Memorial High School, Roger Williams in the 1960s and her grandfather, a civil rights activist and union organizer, in the 1940s.

Willie Lewis Freeman was favorably called "Mailman" or "Government" by all ethnic groups in the Apopka area for approximately 40 years after the mid-20th century, stemming from his employment with the United States Post Office, and most of all, his concern, care and dedication to mankind. Freeman, on numerous occasions, became involved in safety measures, social attributes and legal issues not relative to the post office. Slim often commends "Mailman" through our conversations for the knowledge that he has given to citizens of the entire Apopka mail delivery area. Without a doubt, he definitely knows 90 percent of the families by name in the area. Thanks, Willie Lewis Freeman.

Apopka has produced outstanding law enforcement officers that persons of Slim's era would certainly have known, regardless of ethnicity, for the cities of Apopka, Miami, and New York, state of New York and a Federal U.S. Marshal, namely, H. D. Miley, Fred Risener, J. S. Parrish, Henry Glover, Norman Betts, L. G. Nolle, George Fiall, Herman "Doc" McQueen and Earl Mott, Jr.

Previously, Slim recognized that so much information pertaining to his black achievements would have to wait until the year 2011 to include many persons of our younger generation that should be written about.

Slim wants to thank numerous reputable white and black individuals, who made time and effort to supply Slim's gray matter with such valuable information regarding Apopka's past and present history. Oh, yes! The Honorable Mayor John H. Land of Apopka, considered the "dean" of mayors throughout this good ole U.S.A., winning his 19th term as mayor, shared invaluable knowledge. Mrs. Annie Belle D. Gilliam, whom Slim calls the "Southern Belle," was reared in the area, thus obtaining a substantial wealth of knowledge through businesses (grocery, citrus grove management) and old timers' oral conversations pertaining to people and incidents occurring in the 20th and 21st century.

M. Gladden, Jr., longtime entrepreneur (grocery, citrus grove, laundromat) lived more than 55 consecutive years below the TO&A Railroad tracks. Last, but not least, Ms. Mildred A. Board was the originator and former columnist for "Bits 'n' Tips" in *The Apopka Chief* weekly newspaper.

They are definitely some of those individuals aforementioned Slim credits with an enormous appreciation and respect for their care, concern and knowledge of Northwest Orange County (Clarcona,

Piedmont, Lakeville, Apopka, Plymouth, Tangerine, Zellwood and Rock Springs). In 2011, folks, Slim will see yah!

32 Mildred A. Board Celebration--Robert Board, adopted son, Laurice Peterson, daughter, Mildred A. Board. AHS

The Apopka Chief, March 12, 2009, Page 9A

Apopka had more entrepreneurs

Carol E. Mundy African-American
Cultural and Diasporic Research Center

Approximately 10 years ago, a dear colleague, Ms. Francina Boykin, introduced Slim to Ms. Carol E. Mundy, a very energetic, conscientious, extremely articulate, history buff, and collector of artifacts. She is very intelligent and willingly shares her knowledge of history regardless of ethnicity.

At that encounter, Ms. Mundy mentioned several prominent monthly magazines, and Dr. Joanne Stephenson, director of African-American studies at the University of Central Florida, said she was interested in the history of Northwest Orange County Negroes from the 19th century into 21st century. Before Slim met Ms. Mundy, Ms. Boykin told her she and Slim had access to numerous authenticated documents and photos. Furthermore, Slim had talked to many of the old timers of that era; secondly Slim's uncle and father, Michael and William, constantly submitted information to him of that early 20th century era that can readily be substantiated by documentations kept in a family safe.

Precipitated by the dynamic efforts and time of the Department of African-American Studies at

© 2015

UCF, supervised by department head Dr. Joanne Stephenson, the University of Central Florida, on December 11, 2009, honored Carol E. Mundy by dedicating a museum in her name for displaying specific photos, documents and artifacts of persons, events and places in Northwest Orange County. The dedication took place at UCF's Honors College campus, and Mundy was welcomed by Dr. Alvin Wang, dean; Dr. Terry Hickey, provost and executive vice president; Dr. Jośe Fernández, College of Arts and Humanities; Mr. Barry Baker, director of the main library relative to history of Negroes of Northwest Orange County.

Ms. Mundy informed Slim in their first encounter that she had chosen the Apopka-Plymouth-Zellwood-Tangerine area for information pertaining to Negroes' participation in development and growth in the arena of business, with emphasis placed on Apopka during the 19th and 20th centuries. At that point, it was shown that Apopka had many more entrepreneurships than their Orange Countyneighbors did.

Dr. Jerrell H. Shofner, historical researcher and former professor at UCF, after several years of study, was able to obtain countless documents of that era pertaining to black business owners. He also began having lengthy sessions with Michael

Gladden Jr., who was nurtured in Apopka and educated at Morehouse College in Atlanta, Georgia. Gladden was, indeed, very knowledgeable discussing people, events, places, etc., in addition to keeping a substantial quantity of concrete authenticated documents and information relative to Apopka's people, places, and events at that point in time.

Michael Gladden Jr., having access to this type of information that enhanced his awareness and ability, became one of South Apopka's leading citizens and entrepreneurs, along with Sarah Mead, Henry Terrell, Catherine Hall Yant, Daniel Butler, Jules Vann, Sam and Ethel Green , H. M. Mobley, Josiah Kirkland, Mary Henry, Lemuel Board, Cato Sanders, William Gladden Sr., Epsie Williams, Arthur Willis, Richard "Dick" Hayward, Elizabeth "Liza" Riggins Garner, Bishop Frank, Ella Walls, M. Gladden, Sr., Daisy W. Slappy, H. E. "Preacher" McCormick, Verdie Hooper, Tom Barnes and George Oden.

Slim, along with numerous citizens of Northwest Orange County, thank the University of Central Florida along with their Department of African-American Studies director, Dr. JoAnne Stephenson, for their insight in granting a Carol E.

Mundy's Museum of Culture Events of Northwest Orange County Negroes. Again, thanks!

33 During the Great Depression people did not trust banks, but they did trust Michael Gladden to store their cash in his safe. This is an accounting of money left in his care by Jake Brown and retrieved at a later date. Photo by DrO of original doc.

The Pennings of Perrine Slim

The Apopka Chief, August 13, 2010, Page 12A

Teacher Impacts South Apopka Neighborhood

More than 20 years ago, Susie W. Milsap, an Orange County Public Schools teacher, conceived the idea of a group of determined, concerned, and dedicated women below the TO&A Railroad tracks in Apopka concentrating on walking in the "projects" to act as catalysts for neighborhood awareness pertaining to civic, social, academic, religious, and political issues.

Susie Wagner Milsap, who has taught since 1950 in Northwest Orange County, was born in the second decade of the 1900s and nurtured in Alabama, acquiring and completing the necessary requirements for primary and secondary education.

Several of Susie's immediate family members had previously established homes in Apopka, so she decided to venture into Florida during the fourth decade of the 1900s.

Having graduated from high school prior to moving to Apopka, Susie applied for college entrance at what was then Florida A&M College (now Florida A&M University) in Tallahassee, and was accepted in the latter 1940s. However, her transportation to and from the university in reference to the 250 miles one way created overbearing anxieties, which were alleviated by Herman Davis Jr. He was an advanced student at FAMCEE who commuted from Apopka via his 1929 Model A Ford coupe that was complete with painted colored orange and green images of a rattlesnake, the college mascot, on both front doors.

Herman agreed Susie could accompany him on trips to the college. Upon receiving a bachelor's degree in education in 1950, she was hired by OCPS in Northwest Orange County.

The majority of her teaching occurred at an elementary school in Zellwood, along with several competent, renowned teachers, Mercedes Dixon Sanders, principal, Ophelia S. Berry, and Daisy Belle Willis.

Since arriving in Apopka, Susie has been heavily involved in related civic, academic, religious, and social affairs. When students are out for holidays or school vacation, Susie and several female companions, such as Bernice Wynn, Dorothy Moss, Bobbie Lois McKenzie, Shelia Orr and numerous others, when walking in "Soulsville," would stop daily and converse with youngsters about the importance of academics and other issues.

Being a devoted member of St. Paul AME Church for many years, Susie has held numerous important church roles. One role in particular that needs noting pertains to her skills of persuasion in having young people to participate in church programs, thus enhancing religious faith and beliefs. Susie has been an enormously strong driving force and advocator of civic, political, religious, and social issues in "blackbelt" since graduating from college.

Another feather in her cap of achievements is her significant regard for safety factors for students relative to vehicular traffic and driving speed in school zones at designated hours. Persons whose vehicles frequent the South Clarcona Road school zone notice whenever Susie is present, and they hear her "loud" voice and see her arm waving, especially when exceeding speeds over the posted school zone speed limit or driving irrationally in these areas. The majority of the offenders immediately abate and comply with the designated regulations.

Susie is the proud mother of three children, two boys and one girl, that have achieved tremendously in this society pertaining to religious ministry, master musician, and governmental procurements. Slim has known Susie since her arrival in Apopka and has become well acquainted with her relative to academic, social, religious and civil issues.

A moment to reflect upon occurred in 1960 pertaining to Hurricane Donna, considered at that time to be the worst storm to ever strike the Florida mainland. Prior to its arrival in the area, Susie and her sister Bertha W. McGraw, also a teacher, requested that Emmett "Poolroom Red" Underwood and Slim and families spend the night at their home in the event they needed assistance. In the old days of hurricanes, we called that form of request by your neighbor "riding the storm out" (smile).

During her college days, Susie and Slim corresponded with each other to keep abreast of incidents and events occurring quite frequently in our areas. In conclusion, Slim thanks Susie for her extraordinary vision, care, concern, effort, and time she so ably exhibited. Even nowadays, along with many old timers, Susie waits on Uncle Sam's special "mail" (smile); nevertheless, she is constantly involved with other retired educators tutoring students at the request of Jackie Massey, principal at Phyllis Wheatley Elementary.

Several years ago, Susie advised and encouraged Massey during his infancy period of teaching in Zellwood. Susie, on the behalf of numerous citizens, again, thanks.

Clifford Moore worked at several Apopka nurseries

Clifford "Deacon" Moore of Negro ethnicity was nurtured in Alabama, near the Tuskegee, Nostalgia, and Lochopoka area, where he completed his secondary education. Slim likes referring to Clifford Moore as "Deacon" due to his devoted religious participation at St. Paul AME Church in Apopka since the 1940s. Therefore, referring to Clifford Moore as the Deacon will exist throughout this penning.

In the 1940s, Deacon and several members of his immediate family ventured into the Apopka area seeking employment. At that point in time, most endeavors available were basically pertaining to citrus –caretaking, concentrate plants, and harvesting. There was also work available in muck farming, hospitals, the Works Progress Administration and foliage industries.

Later, Deacon met Ms. Lily Mae Miller, granddaughter of two old pioneer families (Miller-Carmichael) of Apopka, who he married and who was, at that time, a member of the St. Paul AME Church. This union thus precipitates Deacon to become then a member and is, nowadays, an important driving force within numerous capacities at the church.

Ms. Lily M. Moore, now deceased, was well acquainted with two foliage grower/supervisors during the course of their marriage and that enticed Deacon's interest in pursuing working in the industry. After many years of involvement and the study of the foliage plant industry, several owners requested his expertise and knowledge. At that time, Tom Mahaffey, one of the Apopka area's leading foliage plant nursery owners, employed Deacon to supervise his Hilltop foliage nurseries on Marden Road north of Keene Road.

In approximately 1962, Mahaffey sold several of the nurseries including Hilltop to the Stutzman Brothers of Chicago. Although the nurseries Deacon supervised at that point were acquired by new owners, they kept him there in a supervisory status. In 1969, Stratford of Houston, Texas, a large agriculture firm, assembled and purchased several nurseries including Stutzman Brothers, calling the newly formed organization Green Thumb Corporation.

During this period, the corporation had foliage nurseries in Central America (Belize), where Deacon was assigned, residing there to study and nurture some special plants. Prior to his return in

1977, Stratford's Green Thumb Corporation went into bankruptcy. Deacon then was assigned by Ralston Purina, which assumed control of the Green Thumb Corporation, supervising more than 100 people pertaining to production (growth and distribution).

The City of Apopka requested Deacon's expertise, including becoming a committee member relative to foliage and tree beautification of its streets in the latter 20th century. Deacon was included in the four men of his heritage aforementioned in the subtitle as foliage grower/supervisors; namely, Albert "Poorboy" Williams, Elliot Scott and Wilbur "Buck" Chisholm.

As usual, Slim always considered it a privilege and honor to converse with the Deacon relative to botany or religious attributes due to his knowledge and wisdom he so ably projects and gives freely.

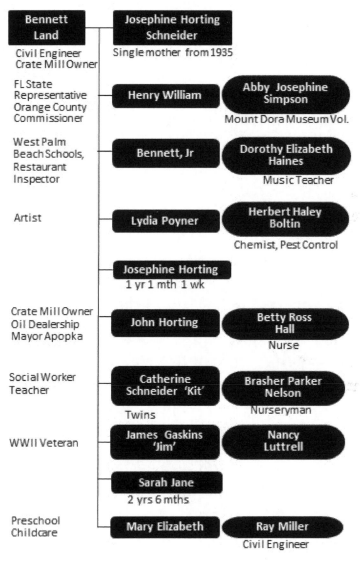

Bennett Land — Civil Engineer, Crate Mill Owner

Josephine Horting Schneider — Single mother from 1935

FL State Representative, Orange County Commissioner
- **Henry William** — **Abby Josephine Simpson** — Mount Dora Museum Vol.

West Palm Beach Schools, Restaurant Inspector
- **Bennett, Jr** — **Dorothy Elizabeth Haines** — Music Teacher

Artist
- **Lydia Poyner** — **Herbert Haley Boltin** — Chemist, Pest Control

Josephine Horting — 1 yr 1 mth 1 wk

Crate Mill Owner, Oil Dealership, Mayor Apopka
- **John Horting** — **Betty Ross Hall** — Nurse

Social Worker, Teacher
- **Catherine Schneider 'Kit'** — **Brasher Parker Nelson** — Nurseryman

Twins

WWII Veteran
- **James Gaskins 'Jim'** — **Nancy Luttrell**

Sarah Jane — 2 yrs 6 mths

Preschool Childcare
- **Mary Elizabeth** — **Ray Miller** — Civil Engineer

DrO 2015

34 Bennett and Josephine Land Family.

The Apopka Chief, April 30, 2010, Page 11A

Kit Land Nelson left footprint in community

Mrs. Kit Land Nelson, Lady who Wore Many Caps in Apopka

It was indeed a great honor for Slim to have known Mrs. Kit Land-Nelson, the sister of the long-serving mayor of Apopka, the Honorable John H. Land. She was married numerous years to the famous O. F. Nelson & Sons Nursery, Inc. roses innovative proprietor.

35 Bennett and Josephine Land's progeny @ 1950 at Mrs. Land's home in Apopka. **Provided by Stephen Nelson.**

On many occasions, while Slim was visiting some of her neighbors near Alabama Avenue and Sixth Street prior to her being married, she and her mother, the grand matriarch, Mrs. Josephine Land of the Land family, he would see them outside the elegant mansion, observing livestock and grounds maintenance. Numerous times, while Slim and neighbors were passing, the Lands would wave or ask us to come in to gather eggs in addition to rounding up stray livestock (chickens, goats, guineas).

Several other encounters that Slim recalls brings back extraordinary memories, including those relative to her visiting my elderly neighbor, Mrs. Hannah Williams, a trusted employee of the Lands; getting shoes repaired at Gladden's Shoe Hospital; organization of the first Girl Scout Troop below the TO&A Railroad tracks with Ms. Mildred Board and Mrs. Bertha Gladden as scoutmasters; construction of the first then Foliage Festival using makeshift booths; and the first chief voter's poll monitor for voting procedures at the previous City Hall and Leroy Gilliam Training Center.

36 Mildred Board, Girl Scout leader, supervises young woman at a camp fire near the Apopka Colored School. Photo from F. Boykin.

Although this article is somewhat late for the present day Apopka Art and Foliage Festival, which was held Saturday, April 24, and Sunday, April 25, it should be noted that Mrs. Kit Land-Nelson, more than four decades ago as president of the local woman's club, assembled the idea of the first Foliage Festival. The Apopka Jaycees took on the responsibility of bringing the idea to fruition and the gathering originated on the south side of William Edwards Baseball Park with several makeshift booths enclosed with sheer plastic materials.

At that point in time Slim recall numerous pioneer Foliage growers, such as Jim Mahaffey, John Masek, Ustlers Brothers (John, Frank, Harry), Tom Mahaffey, O. F. Nelson & Sons Nursery, Inc., O. E. McGuire's Evergreen Nursery, W. T. Champneys' Nursery, Jack Christmas's Oakdell Nursery, Mary Walters's Wayside Gardens Nursery, H. P. Mulford Nurseries and Raymond Hogshead's Baywood Nurseries, all of whom participated in displaying their foliage plants in an elaborate exhibit.

For over four decades, this event has drawn thousands of plant enthusiasts, anticipating many new innovations relative to indoor or outdoor foliage plant science established in the U.S.A. or Central America.

Mrs. Kit Land Nelson! Without a doubt, you've definitely left footprints of success, and we citizens thank you wholeheartedly.

Again thanks for your patience, concern, that willingness to share information that benefits mankind and last, but not least, believing in Jehovah God.

37 Employee presented a watch by Raymond Clay Hogshead in 1929. AHS

The Apopka Chief, May 7, 2010, Page 11A

Clarcona had an interesting beginning

A few weeks ago, while Perrine Slim was traveling on CR 435 and Clarcona-Ocoee roads through Clarcona, it stimulated his gray matter of past memories he had of the area and some of its unique old history that had been verbally passed on via old timers.

Slim also learned much of the city's history while attending the Clarcona Colored School, then located on the northeast corner of then SR 435 and Clarcona-Ocoee Road, in the 1930s-1945. Recently, a convenience store and bank have been built on the old campus near an existing old building of R. C. Kellogg on the owner's property lines.

Kellogg's deep water well supplied water then for the Clarcona Colored School from 1930-1949. While at the school, I have many fond memories of Mr. Arlie Franklin Gilliam, who was from Kentucky. He was a renowned, competent citrus grove manager, avid wild game hunter, and a very politically involved individual who, at that point in time, was an Orange County Public School trustee and board member for CCS.

The township of Clarcona had a very interesting start. The small community, approximately three miles south of Apopka on CR 435, was inhabited before the United States of America Civil War from 1861-1865. Most people of that era herded livestock and farmed. The town was named after William Clark of Connecticut who, at that point in time, purchased a vast abundance of pine and oak timbers for the saw and planing mill that would co-exist with the ever-prospering turpentine industry in the area west of Lakeville, then being called "Clark's Corner," and nowadays known as Clarcona.

Railroading during that era was the ideal means of transporting commodities, the U.S. Mail and passengers by way of the Orange Belt Railroad that built tracks from Lake Monroe to Oakland, passing through Clark's Corner. Slim observed, while on his recent trek, that the old railroad track bed bifurcation that leads to Fuller's Crossing, Ocoee has been eliminated and is now being utilized as a westward county bike trail.

Nevertheless, a portion of the original railroad track is maintained and being railroaded daily, enroute to Ocoee-Winter Garden. The gigantic Midland Railroad water tower, which once was quite visible east of CR 435 just prior to entering the township from Apopka and quenched the thirsty steam-driven locomotives, is now non-existent. The mail-catching apparatus and the depot, then located along the railroad tracks for train's route westward to Fuller's Crossing, no longer remains.

The Apopka Chief, August 13, 2010, Page 12A

More Clarcona history remembered by Slim

Railroad section crew headquarters, equipment sheds and personnel/family living accommodations west of CR 435 and the present day railroad tracks have been replaced by an elegant building belonging to a religious organization. J. W. Cumbie's Country store and the U.S. Post Office were located then (1930-1950s) east of SR 435 just as the railroad tracks cross.

At that point and time, J. W. Cumbie and his daughter Hilda shared the postmaster's duties. However, the present-day post office and general store under new management is located on Clarcona-Ocoee Road west of Lakeville Road. While living in Clarcona during the 1930s-1940s, Steven Simon of Negro heritage was then known as "Steve the butcher" and was very much publicized for his expertise in butchering and preserving wild game meats whenever requested by hunters.

Mr. Wallace, a flying enthusiast of Clarcona during the 1930s, met the internationally renowned, competent, illustrious pilot Mrs. Helen McBride, wife of the well-respected physician T. E. McBride, M.D., of Apopka.

They joined in flying activities and Mr. Wallace established his own airstrip and aircraft hanger at Clarcona to accommodate his Piper Cubs on the citrus grove airstrip property west of SR 435 and north of the railroad tracks leading to Fuller's Crossing. He eventually sold to the Richardson's family in the 1940s and the airstrip is still operational if needed.

Former Apopka City Councilman Alonzo Williams Jr., was reared in Clarcona in the 1940s. Alonzo had an uncle who was affectionately known as Arthur "Clarcona" Williams. Arthur worked as a brakeman for the ACL railroad route from Sanford through Clarcona-Vineland. After resigning in the 1930s from railroading, Arthur later became involved in citrus groves management for Fawcett Groves, Inc., where he was highly respected, competent and regarded as being one of the best in the field of citrus grove management in Clarcona and portions of Orange County. He worked well into the 1970s; however, none of these citrus groves he managed are existing today due to urbanization.

Nowadays, the town limits as Slim knew them have dwindled substantially because other municipalities extended their borders into Clarcona. Before closing, Slim considers it imperative that he mentions a very favorite individual he was well acquainted with for numerous years and was nurtured in Clarcona. This person was a caring, innovative individual who showed much concern for his fellowman. I'm talking about the illustrious Leroy "Roy" Gilliam, former fire chief for the City of Apopka and surrounding fire district towns (Clarcona, Zellwood, Piedmont, Merrimack/Bay Ridge Area, and Plymouth, in Northwest Orange County. Chief Gilliam should be honored every day for his vision and tireless input wherein he made the department one of the finest fire departments pertaining to safety and performance in the state.

Thanks, Chief "Roy," we all consider you the "granddaddy" of our elite firefighting district! Hooray, hooray! This is vocalized by all citizens for the giant of a man (Leroy Gilliam) from Clark's Corner (aka Clarcona).

38 Firefighter Orlando Fire Department Leroy Gilliam. Photo Apopka Fire Department

The Apopka Chief, May 21, 2010, Page 11A

It was a privilege to meet Bob Michaels

Bob Michaels Photos, Freelance Photographer of Ethnic History

Bob Michaels is a freelance photographer who is also a Central Florida (Orlando) native who nowadays resides in Apopka's Lake McCoy subdivision.

Bob completed his primary and secondary education in Orange County at his alma mater, Boone High School, in and around the sixth decade of 1900. During Slim's first encounter with Bob Michaels, it was obvious we had the same thoughts and ideas pertaining to ethnicity, regardless of its origin.

He was nurtured in a neighborhood in which Slim was well acquainted with many of its older citizens. At that point in time, Slim considered it a privilege to meet and converse with this young man who has numerous ways and means of research that has enhanced Slim's attempts and knowledge pertaining to history of Northwest Orange County.

Since 2002, Bob has affiliated himself constantly within both impoverished and upscale communities, gathering ethnic documents and photos relative to the present and past. Throughout several Central Florida municipalities, he has obtained and documented an immeasurable quantity of photographic folklore, especially in a Winter Park area known as Hannibal Square.

He does not limit research to Florida alone. Bob has even ventured to Mississippi, gathering artifacts, photographs, and oral concrete information comparing ethnicity within these southeastern United States. Slim and Michaels have attended numerous ethnic programs or gatherings in the 21st century. Last, but not least, we see one another on a monthly basis.

Bob Michaels gives a lot of himself regarding effort, knowledge, care, and materialistic attributes to his fellow man that has been appreciated highly in Northwest Orange County and other Florida cities. In conclusion, Slim is always amazed whenever meeting persons from the Orlando area, where they regard him with the utmost respect for his expertise and concerns in all neighborhoods of Orlando.

Amos Starbird's plant provided Apopka's water

Water is a chemical compound of two parts of hydrogen combined with one part oxygen by volume or one part hydrogen to eight parts of oxygen by weight. Natural waters are seldom pure, because springs, wells, and rivers are often contaminated by drainage from nearby lands and by sewage from human habitation. Such waters contain some organic matter and the products of its decomposition. However, besides the contaminants identified in the previous sentence, there may be inorganic and harmful bacteriological impurities in water so that drinking water should be carefully examined for all three. Rainwater probably is the purest form of water. Water has a peculiar characteristic of being the only liquid that, when frozen, will expand.

The idea of the utilization of the deep water well around the beginning of the 20th century stemmed from the sawmill operation and its needs for the capabilities provided by a steady, consistent stream of water. The well supplied water for the mill Austin C. and Adelbert M. Starbird (CL&VC) owned.

Conscientious investors, using the innovated technology, suggested creating the Apopka Water, Ice and Electric Company, a subsidiary of CL&VC, which became authorized by the City of Apopka and would furnish water and install water pipes to supply water for public use in 1901, especially through uncharted or charted alleys. At that point in time, families and businesses basically obtained their water from shallow wells utilizing hand pitcher pumps, or lowering pails into the wells, utilizing a rope-pulley apparatus to descend a cylinder shaped liquid-holding container with a spring loaded mechanism once it touched well depth it automatically let water in until the container was filled.

39 1902 boiler explosion destroyed Starbird's CL&VC mill. Boiler barrel is on the right, mill on left, 5 women, a child, and two men in the middle. AHS photo.

When Slim became interested in the infrastructure of water endeavors during the fifth and sixth decade of the 20th century in Apopka, Johnny Oden was the director of public works for the City of Apopka. Mr. Oden, for many years, had the responsibility of authorizing the supply of water from the city's wells and installing water lines throughout the city and unincorporated areas of Apopka, along with areas of Orange County for public usage.

Oden and Herbert Turner, during their tenure, created numerous additions of this same watershed infrastructure, thus enhancing their knowledge and building up their experiences beyond the blueprints (smile).

Roger Woody was hired approximately 25 years ago, prior to the final years of Johnny Oden and Herbert Turner, when all the city's public works operations and equipment were located at Ninth Street and South Park Avenue. Woody was taught by Oden and Turner regarding water infrastructures where he learned the how, why and location of main water lines, deep-wells and shutoff valves pertaining to the entire system.

Although the system has increased tremendously since his arrival, currently Roger Woody is definitely one of the few individuals, if not the only individual within the city's water infrastructure department, having that knowledge and on-the-spot expertise.

Woody, in recent years, was designated water infrastructure supervisor, but due to his wife's illness, Woody resigned from that job and remained with the department in a position as a general worker. Slim usually converses with him on a bi-weekly basis in order to keep Slim abreast of new technology, replacement or addition of main water lines and training of new personnel.

40 Starbird residence built in 1901. 23 South Lake Avenue. AHS.

Alley played part in South Apopka's growth

Old Alleyway Below Tavares, Orlando & Atlantic Railroad Tracks Between S. Central Avenue and S. Lake Avenue Running South

Occasionally, Slim will venture into the neighborhood he was nurtured in, reflecting on various public landmarks that exist even today. This creates curiosity among informed citizens and present day Apopka city engineers pertaining to one particular alleyway that is approximately 12-feet wide and continues for at least seven blocks to end in unincorporated Orange County.

This alleyway in the Orange County "old" plat book initiates at Sixth Street between S. Central Avenue and South Lake Avenue and extends southward to 12th Street. According to the plat book, the alley was established in 1901 to place main feeder water lines in the city of Apopka to supply households or businesses within the town limits only. It was also utilized as a trash/garbage pickup route and a pedestrian walkway that was maintained by the City of Apopka.

Nevertheless, the alley segment between Eighth Street and Ninth Street, adjacent to Frank Sanders' property, was maintained constantly after he volunteered to keep absolute maintenance of it and this was done well into the fifth decade of the 1900s. All alleyways areas beyond Tenth Street were Orange County's responsibility regarding maintenance and accurate location for the plat book.

Robert "Bob" Pitman, developer of Pitman Estates, also owned rental housing between Seventh and Eighth streets during the 1950s. He had a specific portion of the alley closed in order to build additional rental housing that would co-exist with Pitman's other rental facilities in the area.

The southern portion of the alley at Ninth Street leapfrogged halfway between Ninth and Tenth streets near S. Central Avenue onto the Orange County Public Schools' first campus site for the Apopka Colored School in the second decade of the 1900s where, at that point in time, the city limits of Apopka ended. Even today, the northern boundaries of Tenth Street separate the City of Apopka from Orange County (smile).

Prior to Smith's quarters (aka white quarters) developing in the 1940s between Tenth and 11th streets, an alley existed there; however, during the construction, most quarters were partially built on the known alley area. This has recently created numerous problems for families owning properties there and needing vehicular access to Tenth Street or 11th Street, and the alleyway is not feasible for automobile traffic in or out of the area. Most of the homeowners Slim has conversed with shun the mere concept of moving their houses or complying with newly established ordinances.

During Slim's youthful days, those alleys were, indeed, short cuts, keeping a percentage of individuals off main thoroughfares, and to some extent, a good hiding place from your parents (smile).

41 Lower left, Leroy Gilliam, child in front of him is Kenneth Gilliam. Gilliam family photo.

The Pennings of Perrine Slim

The Apopka Chief, June 11, 2010, Page 15A

Early settlers were good stewards of Rock Springs

The First Apopka Environmentalists – Past Stewards of Property in the Rock Springs/Mt. Plymouth Area

Looking back into the latter part of the 19th century into the third decade 20th century, several families and individuals were excellent property stewards, such as William Edwards, W.B. Goding, Mark Ryan Sr., John T. Pirie, Richard Whitney, Walter Schopke, the Stewarts, Nat Ryan, the Welchs, Buchans, and Footes, Wilson Hamrick, Arlie Gilliam, the Goolsbys and Barnharts, Henry Land and numerous others not intentionally omitted.

Now in the 21st century, the summer months of the year are upon us. It brings to mind how important the conservation of the Rock Springs area, as many of the former pioneers practiced, is and we, nowadays, should continue many of their means and ways to maintain safety, conservation, and health conditions.

William S. Delk, a prominent cotton farmer from Georgia, ventured into the Rock Springs and Rock Springs Run area in the middle of the fifth decade of the 1800s, seeking the right climate and soil to farm most sought-after agriculture crops.

Upon his arrival through the St. Johns River and the Wekiva River Basin, it was obvious that the number of surrounding water tributaries leading into what we know as Rock Springs were very valuable assets.

Eventually, he homesteaded a portion of that area, in addition to purchasing 3,000 virgin acres with an abundance of pines, oak, hickory and cypress trees. Farming was his primary interest at that point in time, and Delk designated a small parcel specifically for agriculture endeavors and purposes. The remaining acres were devoted to turpentine distilling and harvesting and his new sawmilling enterprise. He obtained its waterpower by damming the springs so the water energy released from Rock Springs Run's rapid flow of water propelled sawmilling mechanisms, a cotton gin and a grinding mill for grain.

William S. Delk abandoned the area in 1863, precipitated by the United States of America Civil War (1861-1865), but in 1865, Delk and one of his former slaves' son, Joseph G. Roberts, returned to the Rock Springs area. Delk continued business with his neighbors in both counties; however, it is said that Roberts, after a short stay, moved to Sorrento. Delk was very much involved in conservation pertaining to maintaining the Rock Springs area.

Delk was approximately threescore and ten [70] when his demise occurred in 1885. His wife negotiated and sold the Rock Springs property. Thomas E. Wilson acquired Rock Springs approximately 15 years after William S. Delk's demise, thus becoming a prominent steward of the area into the early 20th century. During his tenure as owner, the Orange County Road Commission was in dire need of limestone for building roads. It determined that Rock Springs had an abundance of that particular rock formation and wanted to lease the property for harvesting or purchase it outright. Wilson, being a conservationist, decided against the proposal by the Orange County Road Commission in order to maintain the Rock Springs scenery, as we know it today.

Dr. Howard A. Kelly, a highly respected surgeon at John Hopkins University and a competent, renowned lay minister while visiting Northwest Orange County in the second and third decades of the 1900s, became involved in numerous civic affairs. He was amazed, especially, at the potentials that Rock Springs offered for mankind's educational and social benefits. In 1927, Dr. Kelly purchased Rock Springs, awarding it to the state of Florida and

Orange County as its stewards, stipulating it would be utilized only for the general public's social and educational affairs regardless of ethnicity, color or race.

In and around the third decade of the 1900s, after Dr. Kelly purchased and donated Rock Springs as a park, a conscientious, organized Apopka Sportsmen's Club agreed to lease approximately 6,000 acres for a private fishing and hunting preserve in the Rock Springs and Wekiwa areas with W. B. Goding as its president. Several other notable persons in the area were also designated as stewards as the years passed. Mallory Welch was appointed an official game warden. At one point in time, ASC lowered its membership below 70 persons.

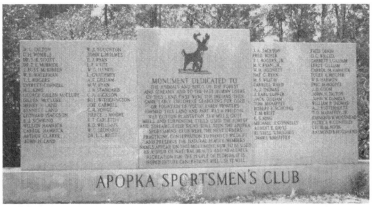

42 Apopka Sportsmen's Club Monument at Wekiwa Springs State Park. **Photo by Dr. O.**

Mark Ryan, Sr., and Nat Ryan, both members of ASC, employed Ike "Kaiser" Martin at their citrus grove as caretaker; however, during the brief hunting season, Ike was assigned daily duties at the ASC camp such as cooking and preserving game that hunters obtained by trapping. Ike related numerous episodes to Slim of unusual adventures at ASC and activities of conservation that had occurred.

Richard Whitney, an influential financier in Northwest Orange County and nearby Mt. Plymouth in Seminole County, owned 30,000 acres in the Rock Springs/Mt. Plymouth area, designated strictly as a hunting preserve during the second, third and fourth decades of the 1900s.

All of these persons in the Rock Springs-Mount Plymouth area were being conscientious stewards with their main goal being to perpetuate an area of conservation and public utilization.

Slim, along with numerous concerned citizens, thanks you stewards for your concerns benefiting mankind.

43 Two Carroll men, third from left, Captain Hodnett, Joe Carroll--grandson of Arlie, Kenneth--son of Leroy, Arlie Gilliam, Leroy Gilliam, Garrett Gilliam, Jack Gilliam--son of Garrett. Photo from Gilliam family.

The Apopka Chief, June 25, 2010, Page 9A

William 'Will' Lee Green, still kicking at 88, was a big-time citrus loader

Past Citrus Field Box Loaders-Loading Citrus Field Boxes by Hand

This penning denotes the ways and means of how citrus products were once harvested in the orange groves and handled by men in the profession favorably called "big-time-loaders."

Slim recently spoke with one of those "old dinosaurs" of the profession, William "Will" Lee Green, who is 88 plus years old and fit as a fiddle. Smiling mentally about his past memories of loading citrus fruit, he readily concludes that he's probably the only big-time-loader with unlimited experiences of that era currently living in this area.

We discussed numerous aspects of the profession and several of the personnel that worked during his era. Will Green mentions that Ike "Kaiser" Martin, a citrus grove caretaker employed by Ryan Bros Lumber Company, which owned large citrus groves on Johns Road just a stone's throw from Marshall Lake Slough, taught him how to load citrus fruit and handle field boxes in the 1940s.

These big-time-loaders whose duties required them to expedite their endeavors in pairs are ancient history: B. B. Brown, Will King, Ben Mucho,

Alex Barnes, Jessie Redd, Beaufort Lovett, Lawrence Snell, James Wagner, Oscar and Arthur Robinson, F. M. Slade, J. C. "Big Jim" Demming and several others.

Even today, in the 21st century, certain aspects of obtaining citrus products once they have been harvested from groves has changed drastically since the 19th century into the fifth decade of the 20th century. New methods utilized today have almost eliminated hand-loading field boxes as it was done in the old days onto a horse-drawn wagon.

In approximately the second decade of 1900, John Pirie Groves (aka Errol Estates) was the first, through innovative means, to introduce a motorized Packard automobile with a cut-down body style from its original assembly.

This created a flatbed to transport citrus products out of the grove to awaiting semi-trailers, and was referred to as a "goat" with the capacity of holding 60 citrus field boxes. Nowadays, the goat is called a lightning loader and employs a hydraulic boom system with grapple attachments to lift and load field boxes or tubs onto the goat bed. However, there are citrus dealers even now that harvest backyards or very small acreage that employs the hands-on effort, including loading field boxes onto a goat.

Amos Starbird's and Bennett Land Sr.'s, crate mill was extremely instrumental in the production of containers or boxes whenever requested by citrus processors for citrus grove usage or shipping, during separate proprietorship initiating in the 1890s until 1949.

Once the harvesting takes place for concentrate or packing fruit, the picker places the harvested fruit into conventional standard citrus field boxes within the perimeters of the grove line middle where the goat will clear the boxed fruit. Then the two big time loaders can load on either side of the vehicle depending on the location of picked fruit as the goat proceeded through the line middle.

Usually packinghouse fruit, once harvested, remains in field boxes and is then loaded onto the goat stacked four high and 15 stacks of fours to the rear of the goat bed. Juice fruit is emptied from boxes onto the bed of the goat. In those days, most crews carried approximately 20-30 pickers, who normally harvested 1,200-1,500 boxes per day. Normally, the loaders would arrive one hour after pickers initiated harvesting and continued well after the pickers departed in order to complete loading.

Man, oh, man! Slim can hear Ms. Mildred A. Board commenting, "Thank God for technology."

Pall Bearers Society provides assistance to bereaved families

Pall Bearers Society: Benevolent Organization

The above subject of this penning is practically non-existent nowadays within Slim's community pertaining to its original purposes that was established in and around the first decade of the 20th century.

Initially then, and even nowadays, the average person's means of financing funeral expenses precipitated numerous problems for families whose income were meager.

Most churches and Masonic organizations in Slim's hometown area came to the conclusion that a society should be created to help confront this dilemma. The society was created with the idea of the society assisting a bereaved family in a determined amount dictated by policy of the society's statutes that complied with the financial contract responsibility for deceased members.

The churches and Masonic groups did not have any input pertaining to the statutes and operational procedures of the society. Many citizens joined and their constant payment of a meager monthly fee eventually created a surplus of monies to assist those in need of offsetting funeral costs for the members.

Once membership increased and members paid their dues on a consistent basis, it was agreed upon that any member who died, their family would receive $250 toward their burial expense. This society was comprised mostly of citizens between the ages of 25 to 80.

44 Former U.S. Army barrack--corner of S. Lake Ave and W. Second St bought by Lumber Company. Photo by DrO 2015

Slim recalls in the fourth decade of the 1900s, the Pall Bearers Society purchased a used U.S. Army barrack and had it moved by Percival Starbird, a prime mover of houses at that point and time, to East Tenth Street between South Park Avenue and South Central Avenue as their meeting facility in addition to serving as a community center for the area. In or around 1990, the building and property were sold to a religious group.

This year, Slim had a lengthy conversation with Roscoe Griffin Sr., past president of the society, who described numerous aspects of their purposes and legal ramifications. Roscoe had fond memories of members in the likes of Letha Burrell, Nellie Williams, Charlie Younger, Sylvia Williams, Joe Cauley, Albert "Poorboy" Williams, Mrs. Gant, and a few others not intentionally omitted. Griffin stated to the best of his knowledge probably only four or five members are still around from the days that the Pall Bearers Society was extremely active.

Former Bits 'n' Tips columnist Mildred A. Board was a member of the local Pall Bearers Society and often said, "that it takes a village to raise a child."

To follow up on this thought, I'm sure that as a humanitarian, she would have also said that at times it may also take the village to help the family when in times of need relative to interment.

Many thanks to the past members of the Pall Bearers Society and their goal of taking the stress out of the events that they were established to provide assistance for.

45 Sammie Smith at Florida State University. Photo Christopher Holder.

The Apopka Chief, July 23, 2010, Page 5B

Local sports figures help lead event for Apopka-area youth

First Results Youth "Pigskin" Combine--
Higher Level Skills Camp and Training

On Saturday, July 10, 2010, between the hours 9 a.m. to 2 p.m. at Alonzo Williams Park in Apopka was held the first free youth pigskin combine supervised by numerous Apopka-area sport figures, including John Hightower, Melvin Jones, and Rogers Beckett.

> Editor's Note: John and Tabith Hightower cofounded Higher Level Skills Camp. Fire Inspector Tabith was instrumental in all the events including this first football combine.

This affair was well publicized through *The Apopka Chief*, AM Radio Station 540 (Roger Franklin Williams, Jr.) and city of Apopka Community Development Office. The first youth pigskin combine was an absolute success and well-attended by parents of participants, concerned citizens, scouts from Pop Warner's Football League, grades six through eight school physical education instructors, and most of all, boys and girls ages 6-12 years old.

Several of the area's homegrown sports figures in the likes of Rogers Beckett (San Diego Chargers),

Olmstead Publishing LLC

Lamar Hughley (Lane College), Sammie Smith (Miami Dolphins), Tyrone Henry (Canadian Football League), Clint Johnson (Notre Dame), Steven Moffet (University of Central Florida), Eddie "Big E" Williams (University of Miami), Curtis Ward (Fort Valley State University football), John Hightower (Bethune-Cookman University), Aaron Jones (Pittsburgh Steelers, New England Patriots), *Melvin Jones (Denver Broncos), and Derrick Clark (Denver Broncos, Rhein Fire, Orlando Rage) participated as professional supervisors relative to activities, such as endurance and mental conception pertaining to pigskin combine activities. Records of each participant were documented for sprint timing, handling the pigskin, throwing the football for distance and accuracy, and how well they adapted in the obstacle courses prescribed by the National Football League.

Without a doubt, these concerned sports figures and the city of Apopka plan to make this an annual event for the area youth. Slim, along with many citizens, thank these God-gifted individuals for their insight by returning some constructive measures to enhance these kids' futures. They are the leaders and citizens of tomorrow.

46 Fellowship of Christian Athletes working to build the character of young men. Sammie Smith, center, sharing his testimony. Photo FCA.

The Apopka Chief, August 13, 2010, Page 12A

Apopkan loved sports

Sports Official from The Ghetto-- Officiated Sporting Events in High Schools and Colleges

Prince Pollard, Jr., was born the fourth decade in the 1900s in Alabama and nurtured in Apopka, where he attended and completed the necessary requirements associated with secondary education at Phyllis Wheatley Elementary and Phyllis Wheatley High School.

While attending high school, his overwhelming desire to participate in any sports created a dilemma because he was small in stature so he could not physically compete with larger boys and play regularly, so his interest drifted towards sports officiating. Shortly after graduation, he entered the military and was permanently assigned to a physical education program for three years.

At this point in time, he spent an immeasurable time studying rules, regulations, statues and administrative procedures relative to sports. After being honorably discharged, Pollard was employed by Southern Bell Telephone Company as a technician supervisor, where he retired after 30 years. While at Southern Bell Telephone during his required 12-month probation period, Pollard tried his athleticism with the heralded Coach Willie Webb of Apopka's semi-pro basketball team, which had achieved notoriety throughout Central Florida.

However, again, he was unable to secure a regular playing position due to his size. At this point, around 1969, Pollard decided to pursue officiating sand lot games so he applied and became certified to officiate sports such as basketball and football for the Florida High School Athletic Association (FHSAA). This activity lasted over a period of 40 years due to the persistence of the late Roger Williams (Apopka High School-principal), an avid sports fan, who was instrumental in Pollard's appointment because Williams considered Pollard very capable and well qualified for the position.

Several other individuals affiliated with the City of Apopka recreation department (Betty Daniel, Jimmie Baker, Bobby Manley, Johnnie Humphrey, Larry Foss and Ray Miller) also aided in his officiating career. During this time span, several persons encouraged him to seek opportunities to officiate sports at higher levels, such as college or semi-pro, including the likes of George Hersey, Bobby Downs, Tom Dorman, Dick Pace, and Bob Blair.

Through his expertise and constant efforts of networking after several years of officiating high school sports, the South Eastern Conference of Colleges (SEC) of Colleges accepted Pollard as the first of Negro heritage to officiate football at any levels of the participating SEC college games. At one point in time, Pollard and Harold Mitchell (State Farm Insurance-Vice President-Southern District) were the only two sports officials of color assigned to officiate SEC college football games for many years. Mitchell, at one point in time, was the only chief official (referee) of color in the SEC football games.

Prior to Harold Mitchell's SEC officiating, he refereed in the Big Ten Conference in addition to several major college bowl games; however, Pollard didn't ascertain that plateau of becoming chief official for football games during his tenure. During Prince Pollard's entire tenure as a SEC official, he was the only official that did not have a college degree or had not attended a college.

Since retiring, Pollard has had numerous offers from other college sports conferences relative to major bowl games as an official sitting in the booth. Last year Pollard was assigned to the ACC Gator Bowl in Jacksonville.

In recent years, Pollard was named Commissioner of Sports Officials, overseeing the Central Florida area that has a membership of 300 that complies regarding regulations, statutes, rules, administrative procedures, and disciplinary ramifications. Pollard has the distinction within the FHSAA of being one of the three chief officials over a period of 40 years to have officiated numerous high school basketball championship games.

Often during the course of our many conversations, Slim remembers Pollard constantly stipulating that decision-making relative to sports infractions create a fine line. Slim, along with many sport fans, appreciates your integrity and your decision-making policies. Thanks Pollard!

The Apopka Chief, August 13, 2010, Page 12A

Apopka was center of most waterways

Migration Below the TO&A Railroad Tracks--Real Estate, Employment, City of Apopka Ordinance and Incident

During the Florida Seminole Indian Wars in the third, fourth and fifth decades of the 1800s, several pioneer families had established themselves in the Apopka area. They mainly came to pursue farming and homesteading.

Prior to constructing the "The Lodge" at U.S. Highway 441 and Alabama Avenue in 1859, the Masonic organization of Orange County held its meetings at Robert Barnhart Mill on the upper Wekiva River. Since Apopka was the center of most waterways into northwest Orange County, this prompted a myriad game hunters to explore the area for its utopia of game hunting.

These groups were comprised mostly of Masonic-affiliated individuals, thus precipitating them to build The Lodge in 1859 in Apopka as a Masonic temple in which to hold their meetings. The majority of social activity for the public and populous transacting their affairs took place at that central location. Immediately following the Civil War, railroad construction became prevalent throughout Central Florida, creating employment, relocation of families and transporting commodities.

Sawmilling raised its lucrative head many decades prior to railroad construction so it stands to reason that many families migrated near these mills. Nevertheless, in the mid-1880s, Amos Starbird and sons from Maine operated several mills for lumber products well into the second decade of the 1900s, and at that point and time, was the chief employer in Apopka.

In the 1920s, the Starbirds sold their mill, Consumers Lumber & Veneer Company to Bennett Land Sr. (Mayor John H. Land's father) whose family operated it in the same tradition until 1956.

Turpentine distiller investors (Overstreet, Enzor, Hammond & Sons, Lockhart Brothers, McKeithan & Company, Norse), after observing the resinous fluid from the conifer (longleaf) pine tree in eighth decade of the 1800s, started the turpentine distilling industry in this area.

This industry began to flourish tremendously in Central Florida, producing turpentine products beneficial to mankind. These industries enhanced the migration of persons seeking yearly employment along with housing accommodations for employees, in addition to academic facilities for employees' children, and last but not least, financial gains for proprietors. Families, regardless of heritage, usually migrated just a stone's throw from wherever businesses or industry would support their livelihood.

47 Turpentine investor and distiller, William B. B. Hammond. AHS

In the 19th century into portions of the 20th century, the races in Apopka resided approximately in the same area. However, the City of Apopka City Council passed an ordinance in the third decade of the 1900s stipulating persons of color reside below the boundaries of the TO&A Railroad tracks. This ordinance also dictated that persons of Negro heritage could not own or operate a business above the TO&A Railroad tracks.

In 1920, real estate and employment for Negroes from the Ocoee area served as a catalyst for mass migration to Northwest Orange County, stemming from a primary incident at that point. Needless to say, the majority of these families were sanctioned by Apopka entrepreneurs, with whom they had previously traded for supplies for numerous years. That says a lot on their decisions to migrate.

Some of those Ocoee Negro families (Hickey, Carmichael, Franks, Brown) that migrated still have numerous descendants in the Apopka and Plymouth locales.

48 The Lodge at Alabama and US Highway 441. Built in 1889. Photo Dr. O. 2007

The Apopka Chief, August 20, 2010, Page 10A

Turpentine was big industry in Apopka

Turpentine Distilling of the Past from the Conifer (Longleaf Pine Tree)

Several weeks ago, while touring the areas of Merrimack and Bay Ridge, especially on Ponkan Road where a turpentine distilling operation was located during the second decade of the 20th century until the late fourth decade, Slim remembered the ancient turpentine still and quarters, noting the abundance of young slash pine trees only a decade from being matured enough for obtaining its resin to distill for turpentine.

Even before he became the seventh president of the United States, General Andrew Jackson (Ole Hickory) fought the Seminole Indians during 1818 in Florida. Timber was very much in abundance, especially the long leaf pine that eventually boosted the economy and furnished raw materials for mankind's well-being in the latter 19th century into the 20th century.

Primarily, trees (pine, hickory, oak, and cypress) had been harvested for building materials, lumber and railroad ties until the late 1880s, when farmers and investors noted the gum from the long leaf pine could be utilized for materialist substances and economic benefits. The conifer is the largest group of living gymnosperms, having mostly evergreen, resinous, needle-shaped leaves and produces a cone-like strobile containing the seeds. Conifers consist of two families, pines and yews. Pines, spruces, firs, larches (found mostly in the northern hemisphere), cypresses, cedars, redwoods, and Araucarias (South America or Australian evergreen tree) are examples of these.

The yews and several species of podocarpus are of the Southern hemisphere. It is believed species of the entire group were more numerous in the earlier geological times. Turpentine distilling endeavors became very prevalent in Florida after the devastating freezes of 1894-1895. The citrus industry, up to that time, had flourished financially; therefore, farmers and investors sought other means of livelihood from Mother Nature's resources to maintain their welfare.

Turpentine distilling initially had a tremendous impact on how the logging industry harvested the trees. Basically, the logging industry harvested trees without replanting and didn't care about other products produced until turpentine distillers and environmentalist made them aware of not depending on trees for timber harvesting only. Once a tree is harvested for timber, it takes approximately 40-60 years before another tree reaches maturity so it can be harvested for timber.

Turpentine distillers and environmentalists convinced the logging industry to wait for harvesting until the replanting and re-growth were approximately 20 years old. The turpentine distillers, in order to accomplish their endeavors, would lease for three to five years or purchase acreage of uncut matured pines for harvesting resin from the logging companies or the state of Florida Prominent early turpentine distillers W. B. McKeithan & Company, Peninsular Naval Stores, W. B. B. Hammond & Son, Miles Overstreet, Lockhart Brothers, Daniel N. Norse, E. K. Enzor and James W. Overstreet worked in Northwest Orange County, Southwest Orange County, and South Lake County.

Miles Overstreet established a turpentine distilling camp at the Bay Ridge area near Merrimack where he and his employees resided, along with all necessary equipment and animals that were required, into the 1940s. Turpentine is a brownish-yellow sticky, semi-fluid oleoresin obtained exclusively from pine trees. This substance has many uses, such as paints, varnishes, and spirits.

49 Turpentine longleaf pine tree with drainage diverters and metal pot. A clay pot sits behind the 'cat head' or 'cat face'. See at Museum of the Apopkans. Photo Dr.O. 2015

Incision type marking is made with a horizontal cut covering one quarter to one third of the circumference of the tree and placing two metal v-shaped strips into the wood for fluid to drain into a catch made of a clay or metal pail. Once the initial practice of turpentine harvesting commences, it takes approximately 34 weeks to harvest first crops; thereafter, harvesting is just a matter of several weeks. The acquired semi-fluid is retrieved from trees by buckets, then poured into containers on wagons and sent to the still for distilling.

Turpentine harvesting was considered hard, dirty work for laborers or prison inmates that these companies could hire for meager wages and commissary privileges to sustain their existence.

From the beginning of the industry, usually companies preferred to hire families that were in dire need of work and living accommodations, so several generations were schooled and raised on the still site quarters until the 1940s.

However, the mass influx of people moving into area depleted the forest for timber, causing a tremendous decline in the thriving industry.

The Apopka Chief, August 27, 2010, Page 13A

Event addresses citizens' problems

2010 National Night Out On Crime--
Annual Event in Area for the Past Four
Years

During previous years, this event, National Night Out, has been held annually on the first Tuesday of August throughout the good old U.S.A., in hopes that citizens would address the issues and resolve problems.

First, let us commend Ms. Linda Lee, who is a longtime citizen of Apopka with deep-rooted ties to constructive community development and crime prevention.

This is especially evident when it concerns the population in the areas below the TO&A Railroad tracks.

The most prevalent items evaluated are sub-standard infrastructures, illicit pharmaceutical activities, the enormous crime rate, and abnormal living accommodations below the normal standard of living in which many of the citizens find themselves. Ms. Lee has, for several years, put forth tireless efforts and numerous hours of time meeting with the "powers that be", coordinating neighborhood businesses to participate materially, obtaining neighborhood churches' involvement and even utilizing personal finances to promote this affair within her community.

These activities are all being done in hopes of resolving some of the problems through preventive measures relative to National Night Out criteria. Ms. Lee, prior to being affiliated with NNO, operated Village House, sanctioned by the Orange County Community for Drug Free Living as an after-school program. However, while at the center, she noted the dire need for constructive supervision relative to children growing up. She spent countless hours encouraging these young citizens to constantly regard statutes (both legal and moral), and last, but not least, shouldering responsibility to maintain a successful livelihood.

This year on August 3, NNO sponsored two events in Apopka with the sanctioning and assistance of Orange County Commissioner Fred Brummer, along with former Orange County administrator Ella J. Gilmore, Orange County Sheriff's Department Sector I representatives, Captain Mike Doby and Cpl. Anderson. One event was held in Apopka at St. Paul AME Church at 11th Street and Park Avenue; the second was held in the area of East 15th Street between South Central Avenue and Clarcona Road.

During the events, the streets were blocked off at 4 p.m. to avert any vehicular traffic for safety purposes. There was a large tent on East 15th Street to shelter citizens for the ceremony in the event of inclement weather conditions.

The organization provided children's games, along with a bounce house, and tables of food lined the street. The mistress of ceremonies was Denese Dunston, pastor of Freewill Community Church, Sanford, with speakers and personalities from the Orange County Sheriff's Department, Johnnie Lee Wright, pastor of St John Holiness Church, Zellwood; Orange County Health Department; Orange County Hurricane Relief Specialist; Farmworkers Association; AIDS programs; medical van for the homeless and the Heart of Apopka Medical Program.

The event was well received by hundreds at both places from 5-10 p.m. Slim, along with numerous citizens, give special thanks to the organizers (NNO, Orange Commissioner Fred Brummer, Linda Lee, Ella J. Gilmore, and Orange County Sheriff's Office Sector I) for their efforts, concerns and dedication for such an event. Slim has noted this NNO event has brought on a petite change relative to how citizens below the railroad tracks address crime and its resolution.

Former Bits 'n' Tips columnist for *The Apopka Chief* Mildred A. Board would write, "Let's take a 'big bite' out of this overwhelming stigma of crime, folks.

Time	Major Events Affecting Florida	
1700	Seminoles arrive	
	1775-1783 American Revolutionary War	
1800	1811-14 War of 1812	
	1817-18 Seminole War	
	1835-42 Second Seminole War	
	1842 Armed Occupation Act –Settlers Given Land	
	1845 State of Florida Formed	
	1855-58 Third Seminole War	
	1859 Orange Lodge built in Apopka	
	1861-65 American Civil War	
	1865-68 American Reconstruction Era	
	1882 City of Apopka Established	
	1898 Spanish American War	
1900		
	1917-18 World War	
	1929-39 Great Depression	
	1941-45 World War II	
	1950-53 Korean War	
	1959-73 Vietnam War	
	1961 Bay of Pigs Invasion	
	1990-91 Gulf War—Iraq	
	1991-03 Iraqi No-Fly Conflict	
	1994-95 Bosnian War	
	1998-99 Kosovo War	
2000	2001- Afghanistan	War on Terror
	2003-11 Iraq War	War on Terror
	2004- War in North West Pakistan	War on Terror
	2007-09 Great Recession	
	2010- Insurgency in Yemen	War on Terror
	2011 Libya Intervention	
	2014- ISIL Intervention	War on Terror

50 Major Events Affecting Florida 1700-forward. DrO 2015

Orange, Osceola counties related

Persons of Osceola and Orange Counties from the 19th Century into 20th Century

According to documented records, the relationship between persons of these two counties of Central Florida date back to the days of the Florida Seminole Indian Wars of the second, third, fourth and fifth decades of the 1800s, when Osceola County had not been designated as being a county in Florida. Therefore, the area was considered as portions of southern Orange and [Marion] Counties jurisdiction. [Different maps of various dates show this area of Florida as parts of Saint Johns, Musquito/Mosquito, Seminole Reservation, Leigh Read, Marion, or Hillsborough Counties.]

At Lake Apopka, when the Seminole Indian (Timucuans) were the most populous during that time, Seminole Indian Chief, King Phillip was the chief of the Lake Apopka Seminole tribe and the Yulaka Seminole Indian village near Lake Tohopekaliga (nowadays Osceola County). King Phillip eventually spent considerable time at the Lake Tohopekaliga areas prior to his son Coacoochee (Wild Cat) becoming a tribal chief at Lake Apopka in fourth and fifth decade of the 1800s.

Coacoochee was able to do this by exerting his ability of fierce warring, utilizing extraordinary wisdom and demanding territorial rights among pioneer settlers throughout Central Florida. Shortly after the Civil War in the eighth decade of the 1800s, many citizens who had ventured into present day Osceola County were part of southern Orange County and Lake County jurisdictions, and they demanded better administrative management and the ability to participate in governmental affairs. Their demands caused the area be divided, which subsequently created what is nowadays Osceola County.

51 Coacoochee aka Wild Cat, son of King Phillip, led Black Indians in Second Seminole War. Located in the Museum of the Apopkans.

R. G. Robinson, a lay minister and state of Florida legislator, resided in Zellwood, which was part of Orange County, but was being considered as a possibility of becoming the new county seat for Osceola County. However, R. G. Robinson was delegated by the state of Florida to take on the awesome task of negotiating between Orange and Lake Counties to establish a new county seat for the area and its boundaries, as we know it today.

Daniel Richard Franks, a pastor and a pioneer citizen of color, resided in the area during the period of time from the seventh through the ninth decades of the 1800s. He resided in what is, nowadays, called Osceola County (St. Cloud) before venturing into Ocoee around the first decade of 1900. Although living in Ocoee, he continued preaching in Osceola County and farming in Ocoee until the second decade of 1900 when a notorious riotous incident prompted him to move his family to nearby Plymouth in order to avoid the atrociousness of the riot.

Rev. Franks and his son Richard Allen Franks became outstanding community leaders in Plymouth well into 20th century. Even up to Rev. Franks' demise in the sixth decade of the 1900s, he maintained religious ties in Osceola County. Presently Rev. Franks' granddaughter Betty Gladys

Franks was a highly regarded advocate of upgrading community relationships for positive achievements in Northwest Orange County for numerous years in the latter 20th century.

Seminole War
@1814 until @1819

Second Seminole War
December 23, 1835 – August 14, 1842

Third Seminole War
1855 - May 8, 1858

H$_2$O melons are worth stealing

H$_2$O-Melons in the Ghetto as Slim Knew It--Farmers of Slim's Upbringing Period

This delicious fruit product has the scientific name *Citrullus vulgaris*. However, it is more commonly known as watermelon nowadays in the system of things.

The fruit dates back some 4,000 years ago, possibly on the continent of tropical Africa. Agriculture scientists have achieved magnificent development through control and research relative to hundreds of varieties regarding color, size, taste, and maturity. The watermelon is a member of the gourd family (squash, pumpkins, melons, cucumbers, etc.). The majority of these gourd family members usually take approximately 60-90 days to attain maturity under soil and weather conditions conducive to growth.

Slim recalls growing up with several men of his ethnicity who specialized in the production and selling of watermelons. Farmer Sam "Parson" Small, Sr., and his family moved from South Carolina and ventured into Apopka through Sarah Mead's Bottom Quarters in 1895 before acquiring approximately eight acres of farm land located north of and adjacent to the present day Apopka

Fire Department's Leroy Gilliam Training Center on Cleveland Street and S. Highland Avenue.

Parson's farming endeavors included numerous varieties of vegetables and fruits. He, along with George Girtman, a competitor farmer for many years, supplied the petite neighborhood and country stores with many forms of produce, making deliveries solely by mule/wagon combination even into the 1950s (smile).

"Old Man" Joe Butler, who resided at the Old Clarcona Road west of the Atlantic Coastline Railroad (Midland) tracks near 18th Street in the third, fourth and fifth decade of 1900, owned a watermelon patch on his property. It was the number one ideal patch for boyish pranks of busting watermelons with a vicious savage fist blow to extract the heart meat only, and last, but not least, stealing a few (o'boy!). Although Old Man Butler guarded his field constantly with a shotgun, we boys assumed that the risks of our selfish objective would override the adverse consequences (smile).

George Girtman, a farmer resided and owned property in Luther Tilden's sub-addition south of Apopka Blvd. between the TO&A Railroad (SAL) tracks north of East 13th Street where he planted numerous vegetables and a variety of fruits crops, including watermelons, for distribution and sale that the general public demanded due to their quality. Girtman relied on his mules for cultivation and transporting his produce to neighbors and local markets. Mr. Girtman's patch did not appeal to boyish pranks, as did Mr. Butler's patch.

Robert "Cuz" Williams, a farmer of many forms of agricultural endeavors (cotton, hay, vegetables, fruit, citrus) in the 1930s-1950s, produced numerous crops of watermelons in the nearby Rock Springs area, in conjunction with Consumers Lumber & Veneer Company (Henry Land CEO) for distribution and sales throughout northwest Orange County and rail transportation to other points of the state. "Cuz" Rob was known for his rocking chair display on the flat bed of his truck, promoting the sale of the famous "rocking chair watermelon man" as he toured the neighborhood.

Charlie Harris, Sr., initiating in the 1930s at Lake Apopka, then on CR 437 and Binion Road, farmed various plant crops including melons for sale well into the 20th century. Nowadays, a new breed of watermelon entrepreneurs as a whole has given up production responsibility, thus relying strictly on touring truck sales within a designated area. Robert "Florida Bob" Griffin, Sr., one of the prominent watermelon touring truck sales entrepreneurs in northwest Orange County since the 1970s, along with his father Johnnie Lee "Dude" Griffin, planted and cultivated watermelons in Arcadia for sales throughout Florida

During Slim's growing up years, especially in the summertime when H_2O Melons were cheap and plentiful, we would enjoy taking melons to our only swimming hole (Baptism Lake) for them to float and remain cool while we swam and toyed with the melons, eagerly awaiting the time when we could consume the juicy delicious fruit. Man, oh man! Those were the days of growing up with boyish pranks.

Willie Fred Rose is a fixture on Central Avenue

The Man on South Central Avenue-- Landmark Person for More than 60 Years

Willie Fred Rose, born and nurtured in Georgia, ventured into Apopka before the beginning of WWII upon the insistence of his older sister, Mrs. Luvenia R. Braswell. Mrs. Braswell was one of the leading female advocates for upgrading the community in Apopka's "Soulsville."

Willie Fred Rose, who is almost a decade away from the century mark, constantly remains active nowadays during his daily early morning walk with his wife, Mrs. Mattie H. Rose, encompassing approximately eight blocks from their home on S. Central Avenue between 12th and 13th streets. He carries a four-foot long stick while walking, but not specifically to aid his walking; it is strictly for aggressive canines to get their attention and ward them off.

Stick carrying by Mr. Rose was prompted from a dog's vicious attack on his wife while she was walking. After daily walking exercises, weather permitting, for decades, he and his wife habitually sat near the public sidewalk in their front yard, constantly greeting passersby and neighbors who cherished the thought of seeing and conversing with the couple years after years. They are indeed considered a positive landmark within the "Hood."

In the 1940 era, employment endeavors in Apopka mainly consisted of sawmills, citrus production, foliage nurseries and Work Projects Administration. The crate mill, then owned by present-day Apopka Mayor John H. Land's family, was the chief employer in Apopka and where Willie Fred Rose was hired. During his tenure, he performed numerous aspects of duties regarding specialized milling.

After the CL&VC mill in Apopka discontinued manufacturing crates, etc., it prompted mill production operations to be terminated in 1956. However, several employees (Walter Chisholm, Frank Green, James E. Griffin, Willie Fred Rose, and Frank Moss) were the only employees remaining after the mill closure. They were delegated with endeavors such as distributing crates via trucks to the citrus or vegetable industries.

Eventually, due to demands from industries, customers were non-existent in the CL&VC warehouse so all new crates were to be manufactured at a sister mill in Mississippi and sent by railway to Apopka. Once delivered, they would be stored in the very large warehouse until the citrus or vegetable industries requested them from CL&VC.

Finally, CL&VC, after several years of only crate distribution, closed their entire mill operation completely, with Willie Fred Rose being the last employee to leave. Mr. Rose a former employee at CL&VC often tells Slim, even nowadays, that he occasionally converses with the Honorable Mayor John H. Land, who then was the chief executive officer of CL&VC, discussing the past mill operations and what importance it meant to the area.

Citizens received financial gains and materialistic attributes for being employed or even nearby neighbors of CL&VC for several generations during its operations. In conclusion, Willie Fred Rose should be commended for the tireless efforts, dedication and support while employed by CL&VC, so ably displayed by sending all of his six children to complete their collegiate level education. All of his offspring are professionals and have contributed to society in a positive way.

The Apopka Chief, October 8, 2010, Page 6A

Centenarian turned on the lights in South Apopka

Street Lighting in the Apopka Ghetto

Amos D. Starbird's sons from Maine, in 1885, initiated the operation of sawmilling in Apopka that later became known as Consumers Lumber & Veneer Company. The mill technology innovation during the 19th and 20th centuries played a significant role in improving a way of life in initially furnishing water and electrical services for the area in the first decade of the 1900s, sanctioned by the Apopka City Council.

Slim, who is at that 80-year-old mark, recalls when touring areas of Apopka in 1930-1940, a person could, within ten minutes, identify every overhead street lighting in Apopka (smile). At that time, only one overhead street light existed below the TO&A Railroad tracks at CR 437 and Ninth Street for the entire area. Project, slum, ghetto, hood, blackbelt, Soulsville – all of those names are one and the same whenever referring to a predominately Negro dominion.

Virgil Blair, a Negro nurtured in Apopka, born approximately in 1910, was one of the primary advocators for electrical services. For 30 years, beginning in the fourth decade of 1900, he constantly appealed to City of Apopka and Orange County officials, especially the dire need for street lighting throughout areas below the TO&A Railroad tracks, in addition to electric service for homes below the city-county boundaries at Tenth Street during the 1940s.

At this time, Mr. Blair was employed by Yowell-Drew and Ivy Department Store in Orlando, a prominent store of fashion in which N. P. Yowell was one of the chief stock holders and a former merchant in Apopka. Mr. Blair was able to receive enormous advice from the executives at YD&I pertaining to the possibility of obtaining adequate overhead street lighting and electric service for homes beyond Tenth Street, Over the years of this awesome task, Mr. Blair received tremendous assistance, especially from organizations and individuals in the Orlando area who had previously owned Apopka businesses or personal connections.

Street lighting in the Apopka hood began to appear more frequently in the late 1940s, but only in designated areas. In 1950, crews began mass installation of electricity for homes below the city-county boundaries at Tenth Street in Apopka that made the utilization of kerosene lamps and white gasoline lanterns obsolete (smile). Hopefully the community will honor Mr. Blair with an enormous "thanks" for his tireless efforts and dedication he amassed while performing that task of acquiring electrical street lighting in the ghetto for his 100th birthday this fall.

Slim has had numerous conversations regarding street lighting with Mr. Blair relative to placement in the blackbelt that was finally achieved in the 21st century throughout area below Seaboard Airline Railroad tracks. The Bible scriptures relative to the creation of the earth places significant emphasis on God's utterance, "Let there be light." Mr. Blair, you always said to Slim about overhead street lighting, "Hold on, hold on! It has to come."

52 **William Edwards, citrus grower. Located in the Museum.**

The Pennings of Perrine Slim

The Apopka Chief, October 15, 2010, Page 14A

Apopka's early economy had influential men

Economy & Growth Influenced in Apopka and Zellwood by a Scotsman

Recently. while touring areas in Apopka, Slim had the privilege to let his gray matter focus on two sites dedicated to the memory of the illustrious William Edwards. One was the old State Bank of Apopka building, located west of and adjacent to the McLeod, McLeod & McLeod Law Firm building on Main Street and the other was the baseball park on North Highland Avenue near Greenwood-Edgewood Cemetery.

The above-mentioned locations also commend and thank John T. Pirie, a prominent dry-goods entrepreneur from Illinois, for employing William Edwards (Scottish-born) in Northwest Orange County in the eighth decade of the 1800s. John T. Pirie, who wanted to avoid the adverse winter weather conditions in the north, was prompted later on to spend four-and-one-half decades of the winter months in Plymouth on a consistent basis beginning in 1892. He pursued specialized business interests pertaining to animal husbandry and was also an avid game hunter in the area.

Pirie, being the primary developer of Errol Farms in Northwest Orange County, has to be given some credit for his future vision of the area's potential growth and economy when he chose William Edwards to expedite this vision. William Edwards greatly impressed Pirie with his management skills in administering to several groups in Chicago.

In 1889, John T. Pirie employed and delegated his then associate William Edwards to oversee all management duties of Pirie's holdings in Florida. In addition to Pirie's estate affairs, Edwards managed property for James Laughlin, a steel magnate from Pennsylvania who had a famous home in Zellwood. Several years later, Edwards became the outstanding leader for the area's development, in addition to numerous civic affairs, in Northwest Orange County.

He also served long terms on the Orange County School Board for district three and was a council member for the Orange County branch of the United States Food Administration that evolved under President Herbert Hoover. Edwards was also very instrumental in animal husbandry research and in the development of certain agricultural products for animal feeds, even at one time, overseeing John Pirie John T. Pirie's Errol Farms.

Banking activities had dwindled considerably in the Apopka area since 1894. However, Edwards was able, in 1912, to convey the importance of banking procedures relative to economics and growth for the immediate area to colleagues and businessmen of the area, such as A. C. Starbird, Richard Whitney, William G. Talton, and several more to permanently establish the State Bank of Apopka.

William Edwards' tenure of being president of the Plymouth Citrus Growers Exchange lasted for 20 years, beginning in the early 20th century. In the second decade of 1900, while CEO at PCGE, Edwards had an electricity generating plant installed at PCGE operations that was capable of supplying electricity for the Plymouth and Zellwood areas when citizens' lifestyle mandated 24-hour electricity services.

He served as president of the newly organized Orange County Chamber of Commerce from 1922 until 1930. A relative of William Edwards operated the Edwards Hardware Store in Apopka until his demise in 1934. Let it be noted that numerous Negro families (Johnson, Davis, Edwards, Owens, Whites) in the Plymouth area for several generations were part of the John T. Pirie's (Errol Estates) development during its infancy. Some of those family descendants still reside in the Plymouth area. William Edwards, the Scottish immigrant, without any doubt, left a legacy of development to behold in our Northwest Orange County.

The Apopka Chief, October 22, 2010, Page 13A

Apopka had many shade tree mechanics

Automotive Mechanics Below Railroad Tracks

The concept of an automobile was noted around 1769 when one was being built by a French surgeon-military engineer, Nicolas Cugnot. This first vehicle was designed from a gun carriage and a coffee boiler. These early innovations relied strictly on steam pressure to propel movement of the vehicle until the late 19th century when the internal combustion engine was developed. Many scientists and engineers were involved in inventing the automobile, as we know it today.

Early development of the internal combustion motors in the American automobile industry, especially when John Henry Ford, after numerous experiments, conceived the engineering concept that the internal combustible engines or vehicles should be simple so the average person could maintain it from a layman's point of view without much difficulty or cost. Also, a German inventor, as Ford had, conceived the idea that owner's maintenance should be plain and simple. Last, but not least, these ideas of both inventors were affordable to buyers and would, undoubtedly, enhance sales for the manufacturer.

Most of the early pioneer mechanics of colored ethnicity gained their skills through hands-on work with motors or vehicles during their infancy period (1894) of innovation by John Henry Ford, Olds, Daimler, McCormick-Deering, Benz, and Buick motor companies, initiating in the latter 19th century into the second decade of the 1900s.

During this period, sawmilling, citrus, mining, cattle ranching, turpentine, vegetable farming, etc., throughout the USA were on the rise to becoming the main ingredients of economic growth; therefore, it was evident that most of those industries would become the principal purchasers of the automotive industry, especially for stationery internal combustion engines, farm tractors, and large trucks. This definitely precipitated the need for mechanics to maintain this equipment, and very few, regardless of ethnicity, had been trained at that point.

Nevertheless, there were two "old" competent mechanics when Slim was a boy that he felt privileged to be acquainted with (1940-1960). This pair of mechanics were fortunate enough to be factory trained at Ford Motor Company (1900-1920) during that early era, which enhanced their expertise, employment and potential entrepreneurship.

Automobile interest in Apopka showed its prevalence during the first decade of 1900.

From 1910 to 1950, mechanics of Negro heritage below the TO&A Railroad tracks included Cato Sanders, who gained automotive repair expertise at Samuel W. Eldredge's livery stable in 1927 and established an automotive repair shop, which was the first for a person of color in Soulsville. It was located at S. Central Avenue and Ninth Street until 1930. Grover C. White Sr., Sam "Red" Green, Council Thomas, and Red Kelly did not have shops to perform mechanical services; therefore, the majority of their services were at the clients' place of residency.

Grover C. White Sr., a highly respected, renowned, competent, certified mechanic was well received throughout Orange County's major industries as an employee for his expertise. Prior to his retiring in the 1940s from the Plymouth Citrus Growers Exchange, he was the head mechanic for repairs over a period of many years.

After leaving PCGE, he and Important Williams formed a partnership establishing a bona fide automotive repair garage in the ghetto at Grover's property on South Central Ave between Seventh

and Eighth streets in Apopka. In the 1950s, Sam
Green built a garage for general automotive repairs
at his property on West Michael Gladden Blvd.
between South Lake and South Central avenues in
Apopka.

During the 1940s, Council Thomas was
employed by Holler Chevrolet Company in Orlando
as a mechanic, prior to repairing automobiles in his
mother's backyard on South Lake Avenue and 11th
Street in Apopka from 1950-1960. Red Kelly, a very
promising mechanic, did 100 percent of his
endeavors during the 1940s in automotive repairs,
operating from the trunk of his car while on
anyone's property other than his own.

Important Williams accumulated notoriety as
an outstanding mechanic, which became evident
while he was in the Belle Glade area employed by
the large sugar mills and vegetable muck farming
entities prior to his arrival in Apopka in the late
1940s. It was at that point that he consolidated with
Grover C. White Sr., as automotive mechanic
partners.

Nowadays, pertaining to automotive
technology, the days of the shade tree mechanic are
definitely ancient history. For the majority of these
mechanics in the last 30 years below the railroad
tracks, most are factory or academically trained.

These modern-day mechanics include Tony Johnson, Ralph Wynn, Stacy Allen, Pete Grimmage, Kenneth Hampton, Benny Bridges, Newton Bell, Willie James, Lindsey Barnett, Willie Charles Bridges, "Pig" Johnson, not intentionally omitting any other "wrench turners" or "computer analysts," who are achieving tremendously (smile). A great percentage of these young mechanics aforementioned have their proprietorship workshops.

53 Author, William Gladden, Jr. at dedication of Doc Tommy Highway
in Kit Land Nelson Park. AHS

54 Rotarians Clement H. Womble and Dr. T. E. McBride honored as charter Rotary members with 50 years perfect attendence. May 10, 1974. AHS

The Apopka Chief, November 12, 2010, Page 11A

Man held many jobs

Sam Weaver was born and nurtured in the first portion of the 20th century in Apopka. During his upbringing and into adulthood, he was favorably called "Bubber".

Sam Weaver Jr.'s father and mother, Sam Sr. and Ida, insisted that he and his sister, Thelma, receive a formal education to maintain an adequate source of livelihood and become beneficial to society with their achievements. The Weaver family was affiliated with St. Paul AME Church of Apopka, which was the primary source of education for Negroes in the first through eighth grades in the area at that time.

This fact later became significant in their being offered scholarships to pursue academic endeavors at the collegiate level. Bubber's early adulthood involved being very active in sports activities, especially baseball. He, in fact, was a superb sandlot baseball pitcher.

Shortly after receiving a formal education, his livelihood pertained to the management phase of citrus harvesting, caretaking for major citrus growers for more than forty years. During that era, he also had proprietorship of an elite café-club, the Chicken Shack, and a billiard parlor. During WWII,

Apopka's police chief Fred Risener appointed Sam Weaver Jr., to the capacity of an air raid warden in the area below the TO&A Railroad tracks. The WWII era had numerous hardship stipulations to enhance the war effort's production, making it extremely difficult to obtain or purchase certain items.

Nevertheless, Bubber ventured to Detroit's auto industry and purchased a top-of-the-line new Buick and drove it back to Apopka. Beginning around 1930, Bubber's interest in civic affairs was greatly appreciated by citizens, especially in "Soulsville," relative to paved streets, eliminating ditches on streets' perimeters, trash or garbage being picked up regularly, overhead street lighting, Boy Scouting, religious programs and upgrading academics at predominately Negro schools, beginning with Apopka Colored School and Phyllis Wheatley High School.

Slim recalls Weaver owning the first television in the fourth decade of the 1900s in the ghetto of Apopka. He would occasionally place it on his front porch, where a gathering of the immediate neighborhood at his request could watch news and boxing events. Sam Weaver's favorite saying was, "What a world!"

The Apopka Chief, November 26, 2010, Page 11A

Organization helps South Apopka youth

A few years ago, Slim penned an article pertaining to homegrown athletes of the Central Florida area who have impacted many civic groups, academic organizations, churches and sport teams.

One Apopka-area group former local athletes have formed is the Higher Level Skills Camp.

It is not the intention of the Higher Level Skills Camp (HLSC) to focus strictly on sports endeavors to encourage our youth to become achievers in the system of things. But, they want the youth to utilize the many experiences of HLSC's members as a catalyst relative to maturity, responsibility and concern for his/her fellow person.

Hopefully, within the Central Florida communities, regardless of ethnicity, it will not deter them from participating in these illustrated concrete programs offered.

This organization was precipitated and orchestrated by professional athletes who deemed it necessary to return some positive attributes they have obtained to upgrade the self-esteem of our youth. The present-day Higher Level Skills Camp chief architectures sport professionals are among the likes of Melvin Jones (Denver Broncos), John

Hightower (Bethune-Cookman University), and Rogers Beckett Jr. (San Diego Chargers and Cincinnati Bengals), along with numerous other college and professional athletes not intentionally omitted.

The concerned and dedicated group has put forth many tireless hours of efforts, financial contributions, networking and lots of dedication in hopes it will piggyback to a percentage of prominence in a sufficient positive way.

In the evening of November 10, at the John H. Bridges Community Center, HLSC presented R. V. Brown, the founder of Outreach to America's Youth program, as an inspirational speaker referencing issues or problems confronting our youth.

Mail must go through

United States Postal Mail Service--Past and Present Methods of Mail Delivery

Slim recalls for many past decades this time of year around Thanksgiving until the second week of December tends to be one of the most important phases of mail and package delivery. The United States Post Office usually reminds its patrons of the necessity of mailing of packages and letters early so letters and parcels won't be late or returned to the senders.

Slim and Willie Lewis Freeman constantly converse as to the ways and means of U.S. Mail processing during Freeman's tenure as a letter carrier for the U.S. Postal Service during Slim's upbringing. Willie Lewis Freeman, called "Government" by all ethnic groups in the City of Apopka, retired in the first decade of the 21st century after 30-plus years of service distributing mail on both sides of the Tavares, Orlando & Atlantic Railroad tracks and Midland Railroad tracks in Apopka.

Postman Freeman was the first of Negro heritage hired by then Postmaster Burgust at the new Fifth Street and S. Park Avenue post office. At that point in time, mail and package delivery was strictly accomplished by postal employees walking to houses and business addresses carrying a harness type bag over their shoulders with letters and packages to be distributed as designated.

Later, the mail carriers rode bicycles with large canvas or wire mesh baskets mounted on the front of them to store mail. Even with using bicycles, the job entailed a degree of walking to distribute mail. Eventually, Jeeps with right-hand steering columns enabled the letter carrier to position the vehicle adjacent to the permanent gang-like pigeonhole mailboxes installed on a pedestal stand.

This allowed the postal person to distribute mail without having to get out of vehicle. Slim recalls, from a layman's point of view, that during the third and fourth decade of the 1900s, there were several methods of transporting mail to the distribution center for the Apopka areas, including the Midland and TO&A railroads as well as airmail letters to and from the E. J. Ryan airfield in Merrimack, during some of Mrs. Minnie Vick's tenure as postmaster in Apopka.

At that time, there were only three ways for individuals or families of colored ethnicity in Apopka to receive postmarked mail:

1. By renting post office mailboxes; only consecutive numerical numbers of the 400

series, initiating at 410, were issued to Negro patrons who subscribed;

2. General Delivery at the post office and
3. Rural Free Delivery (RFD) services "only" at the South Central Avenue and Ninth Street, where recipients furnished their own standard size authorized mailbox. No U.S. Mail was delivered below Ninth Street during that era.

The only other correspondence resembling a letter was the official telegram under Western Union's authority, an area over which the U.S. Post Office Department had no jurisdiction. Therefore, Western Union had the sole responsibility, at that time, of delivering wherever the address occurred in Apopka.

In conclusion, Slim often mentions how mail was processed in that era to Willie "Government" Freeman, although Slim is thirty or better years older. However, when Government recalls the railroad system apparatus used for mailbag collection by catching and depositing the U.S. Mail sacks, he then will say, "How wonderful that era was at the time, along with its technology (smile)." Slim is definitely old-fashioned, but he readily accepts concrete advancements. The U.S. Postal Department–Perrine Slim commends its habitual services in rain, sleet or snow as well as the personnel and their dedication. Thanks again.

55 First U.S. Mail delivery in Apopka went William G. Talton on May 17, 1958. L>R William G. Talton, city carrier Leon Robinson, Postmaster Robert Burgust. AHS

Apopka Mayor and First Lady became sweethearts when she was still in high school

Apopka's First Lady Betty Hall Land

This article came about through encounters with one of Slim's favorite mentors and also a very dear friend, "Southern Belle" Ms. Annie Belle Driggers Gilliam, a board member of the Apopka Historical Society, thus being a strong advocate of history in reference to Apopka and its citizens.

Approximately two years ago, Mrs. Gilliam encouraged and insisted that Slim pen some thoughts about the First Lady of Apopka to the best of Slim's ability. Slim hereby apologizes to the "Southern Belle" and the many readers of *The Apopka Chief* column Bits 'n' Tips for the lengthy delay of the account of Ms. Betty that they have so yearned to read.

Most citizens in the Apopka area, especially those social security recipients like Slim, have had an opportunity to personally meet and converse with this beautiful, magnificent, dedicated, charming and compassionate lady whom many refer to as Ms. Betty. This stemmed from her expertise in the arenas of medical treatments as chief registered nurse for the renowned physician,

Dr. Thomas "Tommy" E. McBride, as well as city and county politics over the past 55 years.

Ms. Betty, in conjunction with her husband the Honorable Mayor John H. Land, established a record for tenure by being in the position of Mayor and First Lady longer than anyone elected to that office previously. They have held these positions since 1949 in the City of Apopka, with the exception of one term won in 1968 by entrepreneur (dry cleaning and laundry) Leonard Hurst.

Apopka's First Lady has several noted credentials, one of which Slim teases her about frequently, relative to her being a "military brat" during WWII. Her Navy-oriented father, who was an alumnus of the United States Naval Military Academy in Annapolis, Maryland prior to WWII, also served honorably during the war. Two of her fraternal uncles served with distinction in the Canadian Air force as officers.

Betty Hall was born in the second decade of the 1900s in Connecticut during her Naval officer father's assignment to study submarine operational procedures at New London. The majority of Ms. Betty's nurturing and secondary education occurred at several U.S. military bases throughout the USA and its territories.

Prior to moving to Apopka from Guantanamo Bay, Cuba, in the fourth decade of the 1900s, her father received military orders to relocate his entire family to a U.S. Naval base in the Central Florida area. They secured housing in Apopka because of its proximity to the nearby naval base. After briefly living in Apopka, Ms. Betty socialized with her newfound neighbors, including one who was very significant, none other than the present day Mayor John H. Land.

56 First Lady Betty Hall and Mayor John Land, Apopka.
Photo provided Betty Land

Mayor Land remembers becoming acquainted with Ms. Betty at what was then the Apopka High School and Gymnasium (currently City Hall) dance event through the insistence of his friend, who was one of the sons of Apopka's Shepard Drug Store pioneer family. [John was in service during WWII and attended a high school dance, thus meeting Betty.] This courtship evolved into a marriage that has endured many decades since the 1940s, even as of this penning.

In addition to this long, wonderful marriage, it is said by numerous citizens above and below the TO&A Railroad tracks to Ms. Betty, "You are indeed an extraordinary cook that keeps you and Mayor Land fit as a fiddle (smile)." During this span of marriage, three children were born. Ms. Betty attended and graduated from Georgetown University (Hoyas) in Washington, D.C., earning a bachelor's degree as a registered nurse. Prior to becoming chief nurse for physician Thomas "Tommy" McBride, she was employed at one of the major hospitals in Orange County.

Most old timers, during her tenure with Dr. Tommy, recall her devoted concern and compassion along with medical expertise, and last but not least, the way Ms. Betty administered those anti-infective shots of Penicillin, utilizing a size 21-gauge needle for injection. How can we forget those moments of anticipation (smile)?

In conclusion, Ms. Betty is as successful as her husband, the present day Mayor John H. Land of Apopka, by being a devoted companion constantly at his side, filled with much integrity and steadily encouraging him onward.

Ms. Betty, we citizens of the area thank God for placing you in our midst for your contribution

© 2015

towards mankind's wellbeing. Thanks again, Mrs. Betty Hall Land; we citizens still admire you regardless of the shots you administered (smile). Some time ago, Slim had the privilege to attend a history encounter that Ms. Betty attended, where she and Slim had extensive casual talks relative to the history of our city and its citizens.

Apopkan became well-known Musical Man of His Time

Robert "Cuz" Williams was born at his parent's home adjacent to the Clarcona Colored School campus in Clarcona (aka Clark's Corner) near the then main thoroughfare of SR 435 and Clarcona-Ocoee Road in the fourth decade of the 1900s.

His schooling was achieved at both Clarcona and Apopka. Initially, Robert's secondary education began in 1947 at CCS under the strict scrutiny and watchful eyes of the illustrious principal, Marie Stabler Gladden.

The entire school facility was physically moved to Apopka Junior High School on 18th Street and S. Central Avenue to consolidate under one school name.

While Robert was attending CCS at an early age, his mother, Mrs. Carrie Williams, an advocate of numerous civic affairs, insisted and encouraged him to take music lessons in Apopka from the renowned master musician music teacher, Mrs. Bertha Gladden. Once a week, rain or shine, his mother would commute via automobile with Robert to Apopka where he would take a music lesson for one hour per session.

The ritual of these music lessons continued until Robert completed secondary education prior to being accepted into college. Robert, at that point in time, had all of his music lessons taught to him by Mrs. Bertha Gladden in Apopka, but he later attended some of America's prestigious graduate schools of music to become an outstanding professional musician/teacher from Florida to Massachusetts.

Robert Williams graduated from Apopka's Phyllis Wheatley High School in 1959 as valedictorian. He initially began his undergraduate studies at Bethune-Cookman College (currently known as Bethune-Cookman University).

Robert received a bachelor's degree in 1963, prior to pursuing a master's degree in music, and soon after, taught music at a public school in Orange County.

Before continuing his illustrious musical career towards a master's degree in pedagogy, he taught music at the secondary education level in Palm Beach County prior to attending the University of South Florida in Tampa, obtaining his master's degree in 1968. In 1971, with a desire to earn a Ph.D. in music, Robert enrolled at Boston University for a period of one year, but climatic conditions that he was not accustomed to forced Robert to transfer his enrollment to Florida State University in Tallahassee during 1971.

At FSU from 1971-1973, he obtained a Ph.D. in music, thus becoming the first Negro in Apopka to reach that Ph.D. plateau of any field pertaining to academics. While teaching as musical director at his BCU for 30 years, Robert continued being affiliated with theaters, choirs, and churches in the Apopka, Daytona Beach, Winter Garden, and Orlando areas. He played religious forms of music or plays when requested, or in some cases, he volunteered his services in addition to upgrading their choirs and plays.

Since retiring as director of music emeritus from BCU, his endeavors entail the enhancement of civic affairs at his old Apopka neighborhood, special groups and churches. One of the present-day chief architects for the illustrious Senior's Progressive Association below the TO&A Railroad tracks, he has made tremendous strides in academic, social, travel ventures and religious aspects within the neighborhood for its citizens. Recently in Apopka, Dr. Robert Williams has orchestrated a nutritional food program, conveying the necessity of consuming proper foods and giving citizens quality meals at various church sites or delivering meals to a person's home in conjunction with the New Hope Missionary Baptist Church.

57 New Cornerstone on New Hope Missionary Baptist Church.
Photo Dr. O. 2014 12 29

It is imperative that Slim reflect upon two occasions in Robert's early life that created fond memories in Slim's gray matter relative to his eagerly engaging in music lessons with Slim's mother as well as his numerous appearances as musical director wearing a music conductor's apparel (Prince Albert jacket) with the long scissor-like tails, tuxedo trousers, formal shirt and bow cravat (smile). Slim, together with the entire Central Florida area's citizens, thank the talented, gifted musician who has contributed so much of his extraordinary efforts and expertise for the enjoyment and well-being of its citizens. Again, thanks, Dr. Robert Williams!

58 1958 Phyllis Wheatley High School Basketball team 3rd Place National Championship. Photo provided by F. Boykin.

59 **1965-1966 Fighting Panthers.** Photo provided by F. Boykin.

Olmstead Publishing LLC

The Apopka Chief, January 7, 2011, Page 12A

Mayor John H. Land takes a look back

Conversations with The Mayor--History, Politics and People of Apopka

Talks briefly held with Mayor John H. Land relative to the politics and people of Apopka entail more than 70 years of history. All of this was based on actual conversation discussed with the mayor, and reflects upon Apopka's citizens and its past.

It was definitely a rare privilege and an honor for Perrine Slim to obtain an audience for approximately one-and-a-half hours with the Honorable Mayor John H. Land just by walking into his office. Slim has known members of Bennett Land Sr.'s family for more than 69 years. I have known the Lands from the time when I was "knee high to a duck" (smile) through Slim's neighbor, Mrs. Hannah Williams and her famous muleskinner husband Mr. Henry Williams, who was one of the most trusted employees of the Lands' mill, the Consumers Lumber & Veneer Company, and an Apopka pioneer family (Morris Chisholm Sr.), whom Slim often visited, were nearby neighbors of the Lands.

First, Slim congratulated the mayor on his long tenure and his tireless efforts at promoting area growth and enhancing the stability of Apopka's strict management procedures. These are some of the things that make our mayor so respected and well known throughout Florida governmental agencies and citizens for his integrity and honesty.

60 Mayor John H. Land and former Apopka police officer Dora Bell Norman hired by Chief Tom Collins. Norman's father was Apopka Police Chaplain and Auxillary Officer Reverend Willie Bell. Pictured at Mayor Land's 20th Campaign Kick-Off. Photo Dr.O. 2014 01 21.

A great deal of our discussion centered around several special pioneer families, such as Amos Starbird and sons (former owners of CL&VC), who ventured into the area during the 1880s from Maine, pursuing the lumber business through sawmilling. The first CL&VC mill was established and located at East Eighth Street and South Forest Avenue in Apopka near the railroads junctions (TO&A Railroad and Midland Railroad).

At that time, the area indeed had an abundance of cypress, hickory, oak and longleaf pine accessible to the mill site without much difficulty, even if transported via mules and wagons. The Starbirds became the chief employers in Apopka. In addition to manufacturing lumber products whenever requested to supply the needs of commercial and residential building, they had interests in naval stores (turpentine still), vegetable farmers, and citrus industries.

Mayor John H. Land's uncle, who had interest in CL&VC at that time, encouraged Bennett Land Sr., a renowned, innovative, competent civil engineer, to negotiate the purchase of the mill in its entirety in the 1920s. Bennett Land's acquisition continued under the Land family's ownership and operations until 1956, with his sons Henry and John at different intervals becoming chief executive officers after their father's demise in 1935. When discussing the mill's activities, personnel and livestock, Slim was amazed at the mayor's precise knowledge of operations, especially actual names of muleskinners and special names of mules the mill owned (smile).

Briefly, during our discussion, the mayor mentioned his brother Henry Land, who was, at one point, the CEO at CL&VC and spent numerous years as a state representative of Florida. Slim did know Henry Land and recalls when he planted watermelons near the Rock Springs area in the 1940s with Robert 'Cuz' Williams as cultivator and overseer.

Former mayor of Apopka, E. J. Ryan, as a young boy, entered the Apopka area in 1880 from Illinois and attended school at nearby Merrimack. Later, E. J. Ryan became associated with A. D. Starbird Sawmilling until he decided in 1920 to open his own entrepreneurship, the Ryan Bros Lumber Company at South Forest Avenue and Fifth Street. It remains operational as of this penning in 2011, with his grandson Mark Ryan III at the helm.

61 Ryan Bros Lumber Company, built in 1925, is listed on the National Register of Historic Places. 210 East Sixth Street. AHS

Presently, Ryan Bros Lumber Company is the only one of the four entrepreneurships (Dr. McBride, M. Gladden, and William Gladden Sr.) in Apopka that has continued business under one name for more than 50 years. In 1884, James L. Giles from Zellwood worked in an Apopka store and later moved to Orlando to become a partner in a prestigious law firm, eventually becoming mayor for the City Beautiful (Orlando).

R. G. Robinson of Kentucky resided in Zellwood in 1880 and was very active in politics as a state representative. He was involved in other civic affairs as a lay reader and the chief architect for creating county boundary lines in Florida for the present day Osceola County.

During this period of R. G. Robinson's tenure as a state official, Apopka was mentioned as a possibility of being named the county seat for Orange County. The name Merrimack in Orange County originated from a river that began in Franklin, New Hampshire. The name of Merrimack Township in Florida evolved approximately in 1875 in our area, beginning at the current-day northern border of John T. Pirie's Estate until it reaches the area of Ponkan Road, where the nearby Miles O. Overstreet Turpentine Still operations properties lie.

Former mayor of Apopka Leslie Waite's parents were affiliated with Merrimack in the late 19th century during his upbringing in Apopka. In the early 20th century, Waite owned and operated a dry good store in Apopka. Leslie Waite and several prominent entrepreneurs in 1925 established the Central Savings and Loan Association of Apopka. Leslie Waite was mayor of Apopka in the 1930s and 1940s.

The State Bank of Apopka, which was started in 1912 by William Edwards and several Apopka entrepreneurs including W. G. Talton as chief administrator, became the main financial institution for the community until sold to Barnett Banks beyond the mid-20th century.

We conversed about our political party affiliations as to why Slim choose the elephant (smile). Slim's family members have always sided with the Republicans; nevertheless, Slim had concerns about becoming a part of the state's primary voting system. Very few primaries had Republican candidates; therefore, it was necessary for Slim to change parties. In 1963, Mayor Land's sister, Kit Land Nelson, who was then a poll supervisor, assisted Slim in changing party affiliations.

A parcel of land was purchased by the city of Apopka north of the east water recharge area on Cleveland Street between East Cleveland Street and East 13th Street, in the hopes of building adequate homes for civil employees. In conclusion, the mayor elaborated on how much tireless effort was made and is still ongoing in evaluating accessibility to city buildings, sidewalks and streets whenever persons with disabilities need to get access without difficulty, whether for business, exercising, or sightseeing. Slim wishes "Old man" Frank Sharp was at this encounter; no doubt we would still be conversing at length about politics, people, personal experiences, wildlife, and livestock (smile).

Again, thanks! Thanks for allowing Slim the honor and privilege to have an audience with you, Mayor John H. Land, your patience, compassion, knowledge, and integrity Slim will cherish forever. Thanks, Thanks.

62 The distinquished First Lady and Mayor Land in 2014 at Sarah Mead's Bottom in the Eldorado (currently called Highland Manor). Appropriately, a homemade sweet potato pie sits in the foreground. Photo by DrO 2014.

Last but not least, with Slim having lived in NYC and being quite familiar with New York City officials, it was a triumphant moment to remember in the 21st century, when the national news media at the Little League National Championship game finals in Williamsport, PA, acknowledged Mayor Land, his wife, Betty, and the Apopka Little Leaguers at the stadium for the world to see how much "country folks" can achieve in addition to having a mayor (John H. Land) duly elected and holding an unusual record of tenure as mayor. Believe me, NYC mayor Rudy Giuliani at that moment marveled at the vintage mayor John H. Land and especially the length of tenure and accomplishments (smile).

Editor: Memorial

The Honorable Mayor John H. Land died on November 22, 2014 at the age of 94 years after serving his city and citizens for 61.25 years.

63 **Horsedrawn caison for John H. Land. We honor and respect this amazing public servant.** Photo by DrO 2014.

The Apopka Chief, January 14, 2011, Page 9A

Basketball player became firefighter

Big John Hightower: The Peoples Man

"Hightower" describes this individual's concerns, compassion, integrity, and accomplishments he has rendered towards mankind.

John Hightower was born in the 1950s and nurtured in Orange County. He completed his secondary education in two public schools in Apopka. Particularity at the junior and senior levels, John was a superb athlete and a conscientious student.

While enrolled in senior high school, his athleticism in basketball was so noticeable throughout the U.S. that many colleges across the nation sought his skills with scholarship offers.

Several high-profile big college coaches made inquiries and offered incentives toward scholarships for Hightower, along with his highly talented basketball teammate Charles Cook. Cook did obtain a basketball scholarship at Morehouse College in Atlanta, Georgia. During this period of recruitment for Hightower's athletic services, one interview that sticks in his mind entails the basketball coach McClarin from Bethune-Cookman College.

Coach McClarin visited his home in Apopka, conversing with John and his parents about an athletic scholarship to BCC. As the negotiating proceeded for a lengthy period, Coach McClarin finally said, "I will personally guarantee that John will earn a bachelor's degree utilizing scrupulous academic methods. He will complete the necessary required curriculum while attending BCC for graduation within the four-year stay."

During Coach McClarin's visit, John's mother, Mrs. Katie Long Hightower, prepared an extraordinary meal featuring "down home cooking" (smile). John said to Slim, the BCC commitments relative to the athletic scholarship in addition to coach McClarin's promise and acceptance of that "down home meal" resulted in John's mother (Mrs. Katie Long Hightower) agreeing to enroll John at BCC as the athletic scholarship agreement dictated.

Hightower's four-year stay at BCC was extremely beneficial to his alma mater. Former basketball player and BCC alumni John Cheney, who is a basketball coach at Temple University in Pennsylvania, said that Hightower's play encouraged competition between other ethnic small and large athletic programs. Editor: Hightower was a starter for four years and captained the team for two years.

Although not officially drafted into the NBA after graduation, Hightower was invited to several professional basketball camps, including the Philadelphia 76ers. After countless efforts to be admitted to the NBA, Hightower decided to enter the teaching profession in Florida secondary schools and consider the idea of firefighting. Editor: Additionally, Hightower taught primary and postsecondary students.

John submitted an application to the Orange County Fire Rescue Division during the last quarter of the 20th century and was immediately hired as a firefighter at Orange County Station E 25 years ago. Several years after being employed, through persistence, studying, strict discipline, and experience, he retired in the position of Division Chief [following promotions to district chief and assistant chief. He was the first black to start with Orange County Fire Department as become a Chief. When he retired, Hightower was the highest-ranking black that started as a firefighter.]

In 1990s, Chief Hightower was promoted to the rank of Division Chief, supervising the entire northwest Sector of Orange County.

After retiring, John and his wife Tabith devoted their efforts to providing funding for qualified, conscientious youth through academic programs, athletic involvement, spiritual endeavors, and vocational training. The projected program [Higher Level Skills Camp] initially started and orchestrated by John and Tabith, assisted by several professional firefighters and sports colleagues, including Rogers

"Red" Beckett Jr., Bobby Scott, and Melvin Jones, impacted the community with substantial results.

Let it be noted that citizens of Orange County wholeheartedly thank you, Fire Chief Hightower, numerous firefighters and local professional sport figures for your concerns to upgrade our youth in the system where they are an access to society and themselves.

Thanks!

64 Apopka Fire Department circa 1950. Bill Dunaway, Calvin Grossenbacher, Mayor John Land, Bill Goding, Lyle Wolfe, Glen Woodward, David Ustler, Bill Talton, Nelson Smith, Les Hall, Mac Walters, Sam Grossenbacher. Photo provided by Land family.

The Apopka Chief January 21, 2011, Page 6A

The Chisholm family placed their roots in Sarah Mead's Bottom

Last Family of Sarah Mead's Bottom Past History

First, let Slim thank Mayor John H. Land on behalf of the numerous citizens in Apopka for reminding its populace of the historical past with authentic photographs in this article as to how buildings appeared in the Mead's Bottom era in the 19th and 20th century. With February being Negro history month, the timing of this penning fits perfectly for the history and recognition of that era.

The Honorable Mayor John H. Land recently brought to Slim's attention the possibility of obtaining pictures of one of the last homes that existed during the Mead's Bottom era that was owned by the Morris Chisholm Sr., family. Mayor Land was nurtured in the early portion of the 20th century, just a stone's throw away from The Lodge and from Mead's Bottom. He occasionally visited the Apopka area, especially the old Chisholm house.

Slim also had the opportunity on numerous instances to visit the vintage home (Chisholm) of the Mead's era in the 1940s

The Chisholm family arrived in Apopka from North Carolina in the 1890s, placing their roots in

Sarah Mead's Bottom, near the gully-like topography of the U.S. Highway 441/SR 436 intersection, near the famous old Masonic Lodge built in 1859 in Florida. Shortly after the American Civil War, Sarah Mead, a person of colored ethnicity, created networking for her race at the property she owned in Apopka as a major source of information for individuals or families seeking employment, sharecropping, purchase of land for farming and built shotgun-shanty houses (quarters) for rent.

Sarah Mead and her husband, Liddy, in addition to renting stables and quarters they operated, also owned a well-stocked commissary for the needs of their clientele. Eventually, the older set of the Chisholm's family (Mingo, Morris Sr., and Rosa) acquired properties through purchasing west of and adjacent to Mead's Bottom on Sixth Street and McGee Avenue.

The previously mentioned properties remained with the Chisholm family heirs until the 21st century, when it was sold in its entirety. At this time, the Chisholm family heirs negotiated selling their property, ending the Mead's Bottom era for Negroes that had initiated in the 1880s. Mingo Chisholm, an elder son of the family, was employed by Amos D. Starbird & Sons Sawmill in the 1920s, and Bennett Land Sr.'s CL&VC for many years as a railroad steam engine locomotive (dummy) engineer.

Rosa married Bill Pinkney and moved below the TO&A Railroad tracks, purchasing property on Central Avenue and 12th Street in Apopka that currently belongs within the Chisholm family. Morris Chisholm Sr.'s, livelihood endeavors entailed vegetable farming on property they owned, and gospel ministering in nearby Sumter County.

In approximately 1937, Morris Sr.'s property in Mead's Bottom had accumulated an excessive amount of delinquent city property taxes that became a very highly volatile and publicized controversy issue. However, many of his immediate influential neighbors of other ethnicities, who were entrepreneurs of Apopka, constantly appeared before the Apopka City Council, petitioning on Morris Sr.'s behalf. They eventually persuaded the council to modify his payment plans.

Morris Chisholm, married the sister of Cato Sanders (Lula), a pioneer family in the area, also from North Carolina. Morris and Lula, during this marriage union, had nine children – Rachel, Allen Prince, Alex, Marion, Morris Jr., Tempie, Margaret, Anna and Wilbur. Allen Prince, even as a boy in the early 1920s, began his proprietorship endeavors involving delivering and selling vegetable produce continuously into the 21st century. Morris, Jr., was employed as a milk dairy foreman in the 1940s-1950s at nearby neighbor Albert Martin's milk dairy facility that's still intact on east Sixth Street and east of nearby south Alabama Ave.

Alex ventured to Atlanta, Georgia during WWII, eventually pursuing the endeavors of religious ministry. Marion's demise occurred at a young adult age. All the sibling girls of the aforementioned family became domesticates, with the exception of Tempie, who had earned a degree (1940s) in nursing at then Florida A&M College, but died suddenly thereafter. Wilbur, who is favorably called Buck, also briefly worked at Albert Martin's dairy, herding cows from Mead's Bottom to the Apopka Moss plant grazing area which was near the Greenwood-Edgewood Cemetery and Page Lake area in Apopka.

Buck's employment with O. F. Nelson & Sons Nursery, Inc. endured for many years as chief foreman until his retirement in the 20th century. Allen Prince, after starting his first produce delivery and sales until his demise, became a household name in Northwest Orange County as Allen Prince Chisholm's "Rolling Produce and Fish Products."

Several children of the third generation of the Chisholm family have indeed made substantial strides in the system of things in teaching (secondary and college); high-ranking U.S. Military; social attributes and civic affiliations.

The Apopka Chief, February 18, 2011, Page 14A

She is a Southern Belle in the truest sense of the words

The Illustrious Southern Belle

Whenever Slim relates to the history of Northwest Orange County, one of Slim's favorite mentors that comes to mind is none other than the illustrious, patient, concerned, and extraordinary lady of her era, Mrs. Annie Belle D. Gilliam.

65 Lifelong friends, Mayor John H. Land and Annie Belle D. Gilliam, at a ceremony to honor veteran Jerry Wood at the Apopka Community Center on 2012 May 19. Photo by DrO 2012

The Southern Belle subtitle depicts Mrs. Annie Belle D. Gilliam as though she is an integrated part of southern traditions in addition to extensive knowledge of the 18th, 19th and 20th century living conditions pertaining to the lands, majestic live oaks, citrus trees, and those magnificent-smelling magnolias (smile).

Southern Belle's family ventured to Florida from South Carolina (Francis Marion-swamp fox). At one point in time during the early portions of the 20th century, the Southern Belle, as a youngster, along with her family for a short period of time, resided in Lake County. This was prior to her parents establishing residency and an entrepreneurship in Apopka during that era just slightly west of the present-day office of The Apopka Chief at U.S. Highway 441 and Bradshaw Road.

Her father (Mr. Dixie Driggers) operated an old-fashioned country store in the Apopka area. This was indeed significant to her gaining experiences relative to public relations that she has so delicately utilized in business transactions, namely Garrett Gilliam's Citrus Management, Economy Grocery Store, and Apopka Historical Society.

66 Apopka Historical Society operates and maintains the Museum of the Apopkans.

Slim's association with "The Southern Belle" initiated in and around the fifth decade of the 1900s precipitated through the Apopka Shoe Hospital (William Gladden Sr.) and citrus caretaking. Slim has the utmost deep respect for the Southern Belle along with the Honorable Mayor John H. Land, because of their immeasurable knowledge of the topographical area, pioneer families of the 19th century, and early present-day proprietorships.

In addition to the aforementioned qualities, both are well aware of numerous present-day citizens by their first names, where they are employed, and how many offspring they have (smile). Last but not least, the previous statement involves citizens regardless of ethnicity whether they resided above or below the TO&A Railroad tracks.

67 Ms. Belle's personal 'Clark Gable' was her husband Garrett Gilliam. 1944. Photo provided by Belle Gilliam.

Several months ago, the Southern Belle was a patient at the Sunbelt Healthcare Center in Apopka for rehabilitation after surgery. Her brief rehab stay still remains the ideal conversational piece at the water cooler among staff, patients and visitors as to the concern, compassion and integrity she so ably displayed while being a patient at the facility.

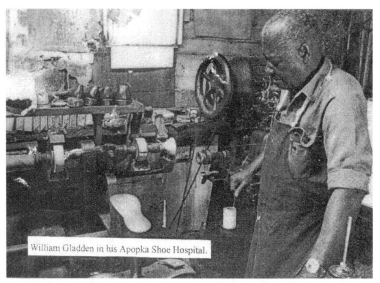

William Gladden in his Apopka Shoe Hospital.

68 William Gladden, Apopka Shoe Hospital, on Michael Gladden Blvd just west of South Central Avenue. Find at the Museum.

It was unanimously accepted by staff, patients, and visitors, which the Southern Belle was completely in charge of the facility during her stay there. Without any doubt, the Southern Belle was in complete control (smile). It is not Slim's intentions to disregard the professionalism of administrators and staff. Several patients at that point in time in the facility were former Gilliam Citrus Management employees who were known to her. She and her husband Garrett had assisted them in numerous ways in the areas of home purchases, government programs, and political selections within the system of things.

Although the Southern Belle is involved in many

aspects of life, she silently keeps abreast of what is occurring, especially in the agriculture arena in relation to production, plant diseases, climate resistance, pest resistance, and drought tolerance. Recently, Slim received some freshly harvested cotton from her estate that she had grown in 2010. Slim was astonished at the quantity (bale) and quality (snow white) Southern Belle sent. Slim thought he would need a hand truck to move it into his home (smile).

In January, while visiting Slim's home, along with Mrs. Mary Hense, an author and editor, we discussed numerous phases of Apopka's history and Slim's affiliations while in Miami with a high-profile police officer, L. G. Nolle. In conclusion, Slim recommends visiting the Museum of the Apopkans near City Hall and meet this lady (Southern Belle) in person. She has the distinct honor of being one of the chief architects who orchestrated the existence of the present-day museum.

"Mrs. Belle", Slim thanks you wholeheartedly for your encouragement. The late Ms. Mildred A. Board, a former columnist for The Apopka Chief and a colleague at the museum of the Southern Belle, would often tell Slim, "Belle Gilliam was sent by God to inspire us."

The Apopka Chief, February 25, 2011, Page 12A

'Mr. Joe' encouraged youth

Concerned, Compassionate, and Dedicated:

Mr. Joe Cauley, a soul brother and a native of South Carolina, ventured into Apopka shortly after being discharged from a branch of the U.S. military after World War I in 1918. Many citizens referred favorably by calling him "Mr. Joe." Mr. Batty Stokes, an acquaintance, who, at that point in time, was residing in Apopka and employed at Amos Starbird & Sons Sawmill, was instrumental in Cauley's decision to move to Apopka.

69 Michael Gladden, Jr and Joe Cauley in Gladden grocery store. Photo from F. Boykin.

Although Mr. Cauley could not read or write, even up to his demise in 1961, he had what the old timers called mother's wit, which enabled him to use a lot of discernment in his decisions. Starbird's sawmill employed him in 1918 as a stationary boiler fireman for approximately three years prior to the purchasing of the crate mill by Bennett Land Sr., who, at that time, was a renowned civil engineer affiliated with the Plant City Railroad System. Mr. Joe remained employed with CL&VC, until 1925.

In and around 1925, Michael Gladden Jr., reopened his father's grocery store and hired Cauley part-time, which eventually became full-time prior to the economic depression of the 1920s. Cauley's employment tenure lasted with the Gladdens more than 35 years until his demise in 1962.

Other than being the chief cook, dishwasher and store clerk, he had the distinction of being the Apopka ghetto's number one church bell tolling individual, announcing many citizen's demise by tolling the number of rings relative to the deceased's age. Also, many families in the Apopka ghetto would employ him to dig graves for their departed ones. Cauley was affiliated with numerous religious organizations, fraternal societies, and Negro Business Men of Apopka.

"Mr. Joe" put forth a tremendous deal of time, concrete thoughts, and monies encouraging young citizens, including Slim, to make something out of life that will be beneficial to the system of things.

The Apopka Chief, March 25, 2011, Page 14A

Hayward was grandaddy of jooks

Richard "Dick" Hayward, Granddaddy of jooks in Apopka's Hood

Across these United States of America wherein Negroes populate the area, this ethnic group has chosen several monikers that are interchanged to describe the area. These areas are usually impoverished and lacking infrastructure relative to what is typical in an area of residency.

However, this ethnic group has found ways and means to entertain themselves especially through jooks since the beginning of the 20th century. The popularity of these establishments existed well into the first decade of 2000. After slavery's (1865) dominance in the U.S., several sources of income became more available to the Negro male who resided in the Central Florida area, mainly sawmills and railroad construction. The previous form of endeavors not affiliated with slavery escalated their being paid for their services performed and set the trend for jook entertainment after a hard week's work. It enabled workers to relax by letting off their anxieties and frustrations.

Eventually, promoters realized the financial gains relative to jook entertainment that people of that ethnicity enjoyed. This prompted jooks to begin to

Olmstead Publishing LLC

spring up near these industries whereas to enhance promoters to engage in that source of proprietorship.

Richard "Dick" Hayward was born and nurtured in South Carolina around the period of 1865-70. Once becoming an adult, he constantly focused his livelihood on being an entrepreneur relative to entertainment. Mr. Hayward arrived in Apopka in and around 1890 seeking employment at Amos Starbird & Sons Sawmill. There, he met Daniel Giddens, a renowned stonemason, who was a much-valued employee at the mill. Mr. Giddens urged Dick to prepare himself financially by saving wherein to become a responsible, conservative businessman.

Along the years prior to his entertainment business, Dick became an important participant of civic and fraternal organizations. By this point in time, Hayward was attempting to locate a facility for entertainment purposes. Cato Sanders's Automotive Repair Shop at South Central Avenue and East Ninth Street closed its operations in the 1920s and this prompted Dick to lease the facility initiating the first licensed jook under Dick's proprietorship. Sometime later, a family member of Cato Sanders did not approve of alcohol being sold on the property that Dick was leasing. With this restriction on the business, nearby properties in the immediate locale owned by the Fraternal Order of Odd Fellows group was acquired wherein he built a facility to accommodate the demands for entertainment. Even today, that structure is still intact but not utilized as a jook.

In the mid 1930s and the 40s, several bars, commonly called "jooks," opened in town and along the highways, causing Chief Risener much difficulty. Complaints of noise, and several serious brawls caused Apopka officials to take action, and in late 1940 several jook owners agreed to cooperate in keeping down noise and to close their music machines from 11 o'clock Saturday evening through Sunday. *See "History of Apopka and Northwest Orange County, Florida."*

70 Chief Fred Risener at Charlie's Place on South Claracona Road. Charlie Holmes, proprietor, center back. *History of Apopka and Northwest Orange County, FL.*

During Mr. Hayward's entire ownership tenure, six days per week, the business was operational as a jook. On Sundays, the business activities leaned towards displaying an ice cream shop atmosphere (cookies, soda water, candies, and tobacco products) especially for the churchgoers.

Dick Hayward and his daughter, Florence, operated the business until his demise in 1950. Since then, several individuals operated the facility as a jook into the 1990s. At one point, it became a popular place for teenage dancing only. From the 1920s through the 1960s, sitting benches that individuals could straddle were placed in front of building to accommodate individuals playing competitive checkers that was a large part of entertainment in the ghetto area of Apopka.

Until the WWII years, Mr. Hayward had a monopoly, as this facility was the only jook below the TO&A Railroad tracks. Nevertheless, the consequences of WWII ushered in Zack Turk (Little Harlem) and Bill Chandler (bar & grill) to establish additional jooks, thus terminating Dick's monopoly.

Slim grew up adjacent to Mr. Hayward's entrepreneurship and was indeed well acquainted with his care and concerns for his neighbors. Prior to Dick's demise, Slim was a Masonic brother of Dick.

The Apopka Chief, June 10, 2011, Page 13A

Apopkan was active citizen in the early 1900s

Relative to churches, fraternal organizations, schools and mom/pop type business Tom Barnes was born and nurtured in the state of Georgia in the 19th century and ventured into Apopka during the early 20th century seeking gainful employment relative to farming and saw milling.

Several avenues of livelihood that Mr. Barnes had expertise and knowledge in prior to his coming to Apopka pertained to shoe cobbling, plant or tree propagating, carpentry, and having an apiary (beekeeping).

71 Thomas Barnes, trustee Apopka Colored School. From F. Boykin.

Olmstead Publishing LLC

Mr. Barnes homesteaded land near early Negro pioneer families in the likes of Sam Small Sr., George Girtman, Joe Butler, John Hickey, Walter Davis Sr., and Lemuel Board, all who had properties that were practically on the Midland Railroad (ACL) rights-of-way below the railroad junction at Forest Avenue and Eighth Street that the railroad tracks lead into Clarcona.

Mr. Barnes established himself as a responsible and respectful individual and, to some degree, took a leadership role in the exiguous community affairs.

In and around the first decade of the 1900s, the state Board of Education of Florida, along with Orange County, assumed the second responsibility of promoting academia and maintaining schoolhouse facilities for Negroes in Apopka from St. Paul AME Church who previously had total responsibility of educating persons of color in the area since the Civil War.

Tom Barnes and Ed Richardson, both persons of color, were appointed as trustees for the then-Apopka Colored School facilities (an old used building) placed at South Central Avenue and West Tenth Street for its academia classrooms. After a period of 10 years usage, the school facility had become so dilapidated due to age that meaningful efforts and building materials used by Tom Barnes to rehabilitate the structure went without success.

72 St Pauls AME Church housed black students prior to public education. Photo from Orange County Regional History Center.

At this point in time, it was necessary to initiate the negotiations for acquiring additional real property to construct a new facility that would accommodate the academia population growth of the community.

In approximately 1927, L.T. Hunt, a real estate agent, agreed to swap a parcel of real property he owned on West 18th Street between South Central Avenue and South Lake Avenue (aka Marvin C. Zanders Avenue) for Orange County Public Schools property at South Central Avenue and West Tenth

Street. Tom Barnes was extremely instrumental in that decision of swapping properties.

Numerous reliable oldtimers of that era more than once related to Slim many years later that they had heard of a verbal proposal to name the new school after Tom Barnes in 1927. Well into the 1940s, Mr. Barnes was an active trustee and custodian for OCPS. He was also a devoted member of New Hope Missionary Baptist Church (NHMBC) in Apopka since early 1900s. Mr. Barnes selected and served on the Odd Fellows Lodge advisory committee and trustee board during the sale of the lodge hall to Davis Lodge #47. Tom Barnes, along with Cecil Ross, initiated a moving picture theater for Negroes below the TO&A Railroad tracks at the Odd Fellows Hall.

Tom Barnes and his wife, Rosa, were outstanding individuals when pertaining to their community affairs, Slim recalls when Mr. Barnes did his monthly grocery shopping, he would definitely purchase a large can of sealed Granger pipe tobacco, he then would break the seal and mix sliced or diced delicious variety apples into the container afterwards sealing it again wherein to enhance that aromatic fragrance of apple blending with tobacco. He admired smoking his pipe knowingly of the scented apple fragrance.

73 Cornerstone of Davis Lodge No 47 erected 1928 stone laid 1980 07 27. Located at South Central Avenue and Michael Gladden Blvd. Photo Dr.O. 2014 12 29

While walking with his great grandson Marvin "Cool" Plowden one Sunday morning on their way to church, Mr. Barnes collapsed on a path near NHMBC and this incident precipitated his demise from ongoing body abnormalities.

Slim knew the "old man" Barnes through Masonic affiliations, citrus propagating, and carpentry.

Thanks you, "old man" Barnes!

The Apopka Chief, July 1, 2011, Page 15A

Law enforcement faced policy changes

Law Enforcement Officers in Apopka's Ghetto Area

Growing up as a youth in Apopka below the Tavares, Orlando & Atlantic Railroad, Slim had an enormous deal of respect for law enforcement officers as to their relationship with the community regardless of their arena of specializing.

At this point in time, the city of Apopka had less than three full time paid officers to patrol, enforce statutes, and maintain order.

The Florida Fish and Game Wildlife officers during Slim's upbringing in the likes of Mallory Welch in nearby Rock Springs area and Officer Walker at Lake Apopka division would assist authorities whenever requested or needed pertaining to statutes being broken. Officer Walker frequented the thoroughfare (SR 437-Ninth Street) on a daily basis driving his 1928 Model A Ford coupe to Apopka City Hall and Fern City Drug Store.

Apopka Police Chief Fred Risener served under several mayors after Chief J. S. Parrish was relieved. Chief Risener had a unique relationship especially with citizens below the TO&A Railroad tracks that even nowadays are being discussed constantly by old-timers of that era as to the chief's means and ways of policing without controversy. Risener was noted for arrest procedures especially when he would advise the person arrested to physically walk normally towards and above the railroad tracks without being in his or any another officer's custody to the jailhouse wherein he would be incarcerated (smile).

Chief Risener's policies and relationships, etc, pertaining to the ethnic neighborhood below the tracks were very successful in obtaining productive outcomes. In comparison to that era, the way present-day Orange County Sheriff's Office procedures are practiced, we have fallen behind tremendously whenever neighborhood relationships, civil rights and zero-tolerance issues are confronted.

The WWII era precipitated numerous law enforcement personnel additions and policy changes. During the WWII era, the city of Apopka was one of the few cities in Florida that employed Negroes as certified police officers by hiring Henry Glover and Norman Betts to patrol and police the ethnic citizen designated area below TO&A Railroad tracks. Two factors were evident in causing the hiring of Glover and Betts: the U.S. Army Base camp at William Edwards Baseball Field in Apopka and the U.S.

Leesburg Army Airfield (AAF--1942-1945) that also housed U.S. Army Negro troops and WWII German prisoners. [The prisoners were transported daily to Apopka and Zellwood to labor at Stauffer Chemical Company.]

Secondly, the railroad companies initiated massive expansion of their existing tracks bringing in personnel (extra gangs) that were 99.9 percent Negro heritage to construct tracks. These special skilled railroad workers were housed in railroad cars in Apopka at the nearby Hamrick & Hamrick Lumber Mill siding. They were usually on a spur adjacent to the main railroad line with complete accommodations, including sleeping quarters, hygiene facilities, dining hall, commissary and galley as if they were living in the neighborhood facilities.

Both aforementioned circumstances precipitated the city to employ means and ways of resolving issues whenever they occurred. In later years, Apopka Police Chief J. W. "Pat" Patterson and Officer Bob White during their tenure utilized practically the same methods regarding public relationships whenever pertaining to the ghetto area as Chief Risener.

Police Chief Tom Collins' administration employed numerous hiring practices of minorities, technological innovations, and social scientist methods of relationship, especially with a predominantly ethnic neighborhood with then-Officer William "Bill" Winegartner establishing and overseeing neighborhood programs.

74 The Honorable Mayor John H. Land celebrates his friend, Rev. Officer Willie Bells' 86th birthday accompanied by retired Chief Tom Collins. Party held in 2001 at Bell's daughter Dora Lee Bell and Ray Shaw Norman's Habitat for Humanity built home on West 10th Street. Family photo on display at the Museum of the Apopkans.

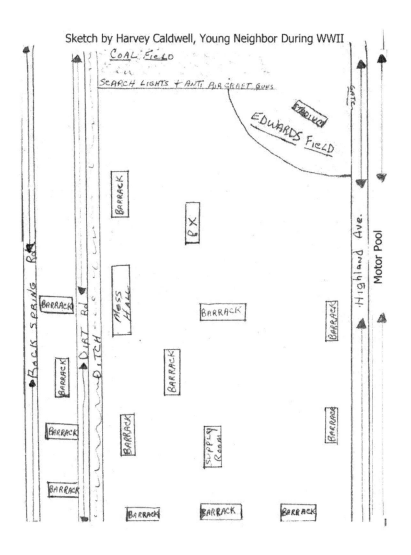

75 Edwards Army Base, Apopka--Sketch by Harvey Caldwell, neighbor.

The Apopka Chief, July 8, 2011, Page 10A

Youth hangouts destroy valued principles

Hangout for youth, especially when youth of a designated ethnic group congregate on street corners in the areas, we use numerous monikers to describe that portion of a deplorable neighborhood, because most of the youth participants don't have any signs of significant reasoning or concerns for its notorious adverse consequences.

Usually, this form of activity breeds gang-like initiation, precipitates robbery or stealing, and encourages rape of both genders, prostitution, illicit pharmaceutical distribution, constant drug use and abuse, and loan sharking. Recently, street corners have become more prevalent for hanging out and creating havoc than its predecessors, namely trees, mom-and-pop storefront, and the park behind Phyllis Wheatley Elementary School.

Well over a period of two decades, South Central Avenue and its favorite cross streets in the unincorporated Orange County portions of Apopka have been a temporary haven for the aforementioned ungodly activities.

Numerous individuals owning property where these participants congregate constantly have advised law enforcement authority of their rights being violated pertaining to noise, trash, littering, property destruction, trash barrel burning, loitering, etc. Bishop G. H. Washington, an aggressive local minister and community activist, at one point in time, along with approximately eight male members of his congregation, would patrol known specified street corner hangouts and verbally, with peaceful language, persuade participants to abandon the area.

Bishop Washington and his men had a petite degree of success. Bishop Washington's group's persistence in persuading these corner hangers not to congregate finally initiated several unruly encounters. Therefore, it became necessary then through the workings of Orange County deputies Cpl. Rick Wisecup and Off. Danny Anderson to precipitate and orchestrate a Neighborhood Civilian Police Force sanctioned by OCSO wherein to aid OCSO as additional eyes and ears only.

This special group would observe or report for OCSO to intercede. Prior to membership of this new program, a large trailer with office facilities was dedicated and established by OCSO Under-Sheriff Malone Stewart at 18th Street and South Central Avenue in Apopka to accommodate group activities and designated programs.

Before the 2008 election of the Orange County Sheriff, the Neighborhood Civilian Police Force project was tabled for lack of interest. Very few qualified people were found after a thorough background check.

It is an absolute necessity that the present day OCSO, along with Apopka Ministerial Association, concerned grass roots citizens, civic groups, and local businesses join together to address these devastating issues that have pyramided to the point of complete destruction for society. Percentage-wise, when comparing statistical crime reports, these corner gatherings have excessive negative data regarding shootings, cutting, assault and battery, etc. Slim has the experiences of residing in several similar ghetto areas that had similar issues in the likes of Miami, Atlanta, New York City, San Francisco, and Orlando. All had, to some extent, the occasion to address issues in order to help reduce these problems substantially to a low percentage.

The majority of these areas confronted with issues or problems previously mentioned have employed numerous methods of the prevention, saying, "an ounce of prevention is better than a pound of cure."

It is very obvious from mankind's history: we tend to destroy valued principles and morals.

[Bishop George H. Washington died on May 6, 2014.]

The Pennings of Perrine Slim

The Apopka Chief, July 22, 2011, Page 10A

Means of transportation have changed in Apopka

Recently, Slim, while talking with Gary Garner, his favorite nephew, it was brought to their attention that, in Apopka, no longer are there any interstate bus stations, train station depots, waterways docks, slips and wharfs that previously were means and ways for interstate travel in and out of Apopka.

Actually, they were more stops versus stations. At these stops, you could purchase tickets, but accommodations, if they were available, were meager. None of these stops operated 24-hours a day seven days a week, therefore, it became necessary to be concerned about available business hours in order to utilize the scheduled stops.

Traveling usage at the majority of these stops was at a very low level and there were very few late scheduled stops. Slim recalls periods relative to traveling during his upbringing when at one point in time, only one bus carrier (Florida Motor Lines) had the entire franchise for Florida interstate travel. The old U.S. Highway 441 from Orlando to Apopka then involved Apopka Boulevard and Alabama Avenue for buses traveling northwest to other locations in Florida and would travel through Apopka.

Their first stop then was where Wombles and Al

Davis operated a Gulf gas station, store, and automotive garage on the corner of U.S. 441 (now called Fred Dunn Sr. Highway) and Alabama Avenue near the historical Masonic Temple.

The second bus stop in those days in Apopka was Lasater's Automotive & Aircraft Garage located at Central Avenue and U.S. 441. It had an unusual aircraft hangar-shaped building wherein Lasater occasionally repaired airplanes and sold bus tickets.

Since that era, several locations have been established as bus stops but the Fourth Street and U.S. 441 stop Slim considered the most efficient in complying with interstate travel statutes. Late in the 1940s, a nationwide carrier, Greyhound Lines, acquired complete control of Florida Motor Lines, terminating its monopoly on interstate traveling in Florida.

Some years later, Trailways Bus Lines (aka "Big Red") also operated throughout Florida.

In conclusion, regarding the interstate bus routes, let's not forget the past when buses traveled most major highways, and you stood on the right of way and flagged it down for transportation to most destinations, thus paying or acquiring a ticket when arriving at the next major stop (smile).

Railway transportation of the mid-20th century held a prevalent position within interstate traveling.

The Pennings of Perrine Slim

Here in Apopka, in the early 1900s, it was proposed that one railroad station depot be constructed for both railroad companies at the railroad junction of existing railroad companies crossover lines, namely the Midland (ACL) and the TO&A Railroad (SAL) locale at East Eighth Street and South Forest Avenue. Nevertheless, each company decided to construct a complete accommodation station depot of their own at other locations. The Midland (ACL) station was at the northeast corner of U.S. 441 and Forest Avenue, while the TO&A (SAL) was on East Sixth Street and Station Street between South Park Avenue and South Central Avenue.

Passenger travel was more convenient, especially when riding the SAL, due to its stops between Wildwood and Orlando. Even into the fifth decade of the 1900s, the above two railroad carriers had passenger service. Presently, the SAL station depot adjacent to its mainline railroad tracks is the only remaining station of two built in the area but is no longer affiliated with the railroad business, and it is being utilized for no purpose.

76 Railroad station on Station Street on the northside of the TO&A Railroad. Seaboard Air Line Railway Passenger Depot built 1918. This was one was rebuilt after the 1918 windstorm that destroyed the more elaborate 1885ish depot. AHS

The St. Johns River in Florida is more than 300 miles long from its origin flowing northeastward through most of Central Florida into the Atlantic Ocean near Jacksonville and has numerous large and small river tributaries (Ocklawaha, Wekiva, Econlockhatchee) that flow into the St. Johns, especially in the Central Florida region wherein most are accessible to large bodies of surface water, creating connecting waterway highways for vessels and passengers' travels.

Lake Apopka's vast acreage at that point in time made it the second largest fresh water lake in Florida, and it was near those ideal chains of waterways that entrepreneurs along the banks near villages, settlements, or major ports of entry constructed landing docks, slips, piers and wharfs for passengers' transportation accommodations, commercial fishing camps, and shipping and receiving commodities endeavors.

Riverboat travel into Sanford's Lake Monroe port was, at one point in time, the number one mode of transportation for traveling into the interior of Central Florida for seeking employment. It was also an affordable means of moving a household, acquiring a homestead, and purchasing land. These examples are some of the good ole days of Apopka's pioneer families' travels. The illustrious and honorable Mayor John H. Land and Slim agree that these experiences made Apopka worth bragging about. That is especially true whenever the muleskinners handled mules involving clearing land adjacent to the riverbanks or shorelines, pulling harvested logs out of river for riverboat fuel and occasionally pulling riverboats through unnavigable waterways. That is why they certainly were a sight to hear and see because muleskinners had a language of their own that humans do not understand (smile).

The Apopka Chief, July 29, 2011, Page 10A

Is economy causing us to revert back to quarters-type accommodations?

Prior to the 21st century, it was definitely a trend for families to purchase a home if their financial background dictated. I hope that as the above subtitle prophesied, that will not be a reality anytime soon or ever. Later on in this penning Slim reflects on concrete information verbally received from responsible elders and Slim's personal knowledge of quarters accommodations wherein the reader will grasp about quarters-type living.

Nowadays, since 2005 within the home-housing market, purchasing has reached a peak of decline precipitated by many potential buyers' inability to maintain their mortgage contract, resulting in enormous numbers of foreclosures. These daily events of massive foreclosures throughout our country have been forced by cataclysmic actions of unemployment over long extended periods of time.

The idea of quarters for living accommodations became synonymous with the housing of slaves on a plantation. After slavery, several industrial companies (turpentine, sawmilling and farming) adopted the method of housing their employees in quarters facilities.

In the late 1890's, a great number of Negroes

migrated into Apopka through several waterways on riverboats or barges into Clay Springs, the Wekiva River, Lake Apopka or Oklawaha River. Their next stop usually was Mead's bottom to locate housing, seek employment, homesteading, sharecropping and purchasing of land.

Sarah Mead, a female of color, owned and managed several shacks known as "Mead's Bottom Quarters" in addition to a lucrative commissary and made them available to the newcomers.

77 Talton quarters on Washington Avenue between Michael Gladden Blvd and 10th Street. Photo by DrO 2015

Numerous conversations that Slim had with Michael Gladden, for whom Michael Gladden Blvd. (formerly 9th St.) was named, indicated that the Gladden family lived there for a period of time upon arrival in the Apopka area. He frequently mentioned that the shacks were made available but there were many adverse social and health conditions existent in the quarters during that period. Most of the shacks were constructed out of pine tree slabs that the planing mill had discarded. However, these slabs were well suited for construction of the simple shacks and, last but not least, the lumber material was free for the asking and taking at the mill site.

Construction usually consisted of one room, occasionally a window, one-door, and dirt floors. These shacks were commonly referred to as shotgun houses because they resembled looking down the barrel of a 12-gauge shotgun (smile).

Michael Gladden recalled many nights when he and his brother William Gladden, while lying down, could gaze upward and count the stars in the sky. This was because most of the roofs of these homes were not completely closed to the elements.

Mead's Bottom Quarters served more so as a staging area for families while waiting to purchase property for homes or farms. The lumber mills such as Starbird, Hamrick & Hamrick, and CL&VC all furnished quarters for their employees. These quarters were usually on the mill site, however, Hamrick & Hamrick had additional housing quarters on Tenth Street between Lake and Washington avenues, which they later sold to the employees.

There were also two other female-of-color entrepreneurs who had housing located in the Apopka area. Mrs. Ella Walls had property that was located on S. Park Avenue between 11th and 12th Streets and had many shacks in her quarters that supported her livelihood. Mrs. Mary Henry, another female entrepreneur renting quarters, was located at S. Central and 12th Street and even in present day 2011 Mrs. Henry's original home site remains as a reminder of the quarters. On the old Clarcona Road and 13th Street there were quarters known as the "Longhouse Quarters" due to their shape. These housed several families who were employed by the veneer mill.

78 Longhouse, unlike shotgun houses, the doors were not on opposite ends of the building 214 E 12th St (built 1930). Photo Dr. O. 2015 01

As population increased, landowners and real estate developers began to visualize the financial gain in the housing market, so they invested more into building more quarters or meager homes to support the influx of migrants.

L. T. Hunt, a real estate broker from Longwood, played a significant role in the development and improvement of the quarters, homes and land sales to persons who normally could not afford them. Brown quarters (Foggy Bottom quarters) were located at Apopka-Ocoee Road near Bradshaw Rd. and they were built in the early 1940s.

79 Foggy Bottom quarters. Ocoee-Apopka Road and Bradshaw.
Photo Dr.O. 2015 01

In many cases, tenants rented to own provided that they could not purchase them initially. Better than 95% of the original homes are still standing today (2011) and are occupied by their owners.

White quarters, as they were called because of their color, were located at S. Central and Tenth Street in Apopka and promoted by Midland Railroad steam locomotive engineer Smith, a native of Apopka, in the forties with the same concept of rent to buy. Slim recalls when some tenants paid less than $2.50 per week that contributed towards the interest and principal to pay off the debt on the home. When they were built, there were approximately a dozen of them built. As of today, fewer than four of them remain. Red quarters, as they were known, were located on 13th street between S. Central and Lake Avenue and were available on a rental basis. However, these quarters had quite a bit of history to talk about that came about during their existence.

Albert Boykin Sr. who resided there in the early 1940s was an activist for the labor union involving the mills. At that time, unionization was a very hot issue for the workers at the mills, and this created numerous issues and conflicts around the quarters relative to this subject. Red quarters were also known as the "Miss Dolly" quarters and, as of this writing in 2011, none of the footprints of the Red quarters exist in Apopka.

The "Graveyard Juke Quarters" were rental properties that came as a result of the need for temporary housing to support the workers that were involved in muck farming, harvesting and cultivating during that season. These quarters were known to house a number of riff-raff and were notorious from

Florida to New York along the entire Eastern Seaboard coastline for its irregularities. These quarters were later replaced with the housing that came to be known as "Hawthorne Village Apartments".

As of the writing (2011) of this article, that complex has been demolished. Nowadays, the trend in Apopka is to lease or purchase single-family housing if you can afford it (smile). Indeed we have come a long way from the "shotgun house", and thank God for that insight and blessing.

The Apopka Chief, August 5, 2011, Page 7A

Masculinity and femininity a constant teaching necessity

Soul Brother and Soul Sister, Born Free that is the Way it's Supposed to be.

Changes about them are hard to comprehend unless you actually experience living in the area or spend a significant deal of time doing research in the area that has monikers or aliases such as the 'hood, project, ghetto, bottom, slums, soulsville, and "black belt" (all areas are one and the same).

Relative to the subject of this article, "Violence among teenagers and young adults" in Apopka nowadays has, without a doubt, gotten beyond society's control. This has caused tremendous, devastating problems affecting all society due mainly to events such as senseless killings, home invasions, uttering instruments, rape and robbery. Many of these incidents are performed for insignificant reasons and, in some cases, just to satisfy their personal whims.

The era being referenced is responsible for those females and males being born during the ending of the 1980s through 2008. This group of youth has percentages of incidents that are extremely high. They automatically disregard the few scruples they have by completely disobeying Jehovah God's laws pertaining to morals and principles. This may stem primarily

© 2015

from the fact that their parent(s) throughout conception and adolescent periods failed to instill in these kids, basic morals and principles wherein they would be aware of the negative aspects that occur as a result of their actions and the basic tenets of obeying Jehovah God's laws.

In Apopka, in these physical areas previously mentioned, there are numerous excruciating factors that precipitate these youths' behavioral patterns on a daily basis. Whenever a youth does not conform to strict morals and principles, especially in the arena of illicit pharmaceutical activities (sales, abuse or use), lack of educational skills, uncontrollable alcohol abuse, ways and means of personal welfare, including robbery, stealing, dependency on parents, grandparents, girlfriends, con-man attributes or prostitution, very often the surrounding area can be the reason for this young person acting out as they do at times.

Without a doubt in most social scientists' research data, families of the past 75-100 years indeed had much more cohesive qualities as family units. There was, without a doubt, especially with the mother, a physical feeding-bonding stage. Mothers of today do not apply that technique whereas to act as a catalyst to enhance the child's learning ability for the respect of morals and principles to the extent very little deviation can exist.

One key aspect of family life during that heretofore mentioned era pertains to the fact that both parents were available 24/7 during the upbringing of their offspring. They were constantly aware of instructing their offspring and rarely were families with more than one child who did not have the same father.

Nowadays, that trend tends to be disregarded due to single parenting. Therefore, the average single-parent family consists of multiple fathers at these dwellings with an alarming rate of constant practice. It stands to reason that this is why the majority of our states' legal systems have numerous child support cases to legally force deadbeat fathers to assume financial responsibility resulting from DNA data. Even with this economical approach, there is an absolute necessity for the child's father to be constantly involved in their nurturing throughout the childhood and adolescent stages of one's life.

There are many households that have been successful with only a single parent. However, only a minimum percentage of these single parents are capable of molding completeness, especially when pertaining to boys.

Nevertheless, there is a dire need for total instructions wherein that characteristic of masculinity is embedded within their gray matter, along with responsibility, morals, and principles.

Boys or girls, nowadays, whenever instructed by strict masculine or feminine ways of life regarding morals and principles, tend to relish the thought of someone's concern and caring, therefore, its influence is part of their behavioral patterns to conform to doing the things that are right in the sight of Jehovah God. They are also self-satisfying wherein they don't stray from the basic teaching of morals and principles by concerned parents and concerned citizens.

Many of you young soul sisters and soul brothers have continuously read Slim's writing in The Apopka Chief column Bits 'n' Tips over the masculinity and femininity a constant teaching necessity years, especially one article created by a colleague of mine, Ms. Francina Boykin: "The black man done come off the chain." Therefore, Slim positively assured that the intent of that lifestyle should have created a positive way of action and ways to offset the negative form of lifestyles that the majority of young males and females in Apopka tend to emulate with delight and disregard for mankind. Too many young females and males of Slim's race are definitely a nuisance to themselves and society by steadily degrading her or his ethnicity without reservations.

Most young soul sisters and soul brothers of

Apopka that Slim is penning about assume to have a tendency relative to narcissism that eventually precipitates being incarcerated or one time only through the undertaker's doors (cemetery bound).

The Apopka Chief, August 19, 2011, Page 12A

In spite of wrong decisions, there is hope for youth

Lack of Strict Parental Guidance

Recently, Slim penned an article pertaining exclusively to the Negro male youth in Apopka having a high disregard for the tenet so ably given to mankind by Jehovah God for his love and kindness. Slim intentionally omitted their counterpart, the Negro female youth of Apopka that definitely needs to be addressed for their role in undermining the morals and principles set forth by Jehovah God and specially delivered by Moses, God's messenger.

It is an absolute necessity to maintain a vigilance regarding basic wisdom and your gray matter ability. Daily decisions are made that we consider being minor, however, there's a probability that circumstances could affect our morals and principles to the extent that our perceptive thoughts will not distinguish good from bad whenever relating to principles and morals we contemplate disobeying in order for selfish reasons to satisfy self-gratification.

When observing the Negro female youth, Slim's thoughts reflect upon his elementary teacher's instructions relative especially to the female youth.

The teacher utilized the old-fashioned Coca-Cola bottles' characteristic streamlined shape as an example. Girls, Jehovah God has blessed your body and physique with all the aspects of beauty and shape, therefore, be aware to ascertain in your gray matter thoroughly the decisions you make in regards to your body (temple).

The majority of our ethnic (Negro) female youth in Apopka have a tendency to strongly advocate materialistic avenues of being approved by society, not by Jehovah God, ignoring his tenet and their own self-esteem. This, often times, causes them to host numerous arenas of illicit activities, namely pharmaceutical drugs (sales or use), shoplifting, prostitution, truancy, alcohol consumption, home invasions, stealing, armed robbery, uttering instruments, etc.

There is an elevated disregard for these female youths' needs and wants relative to economic factors that become a portion of the equation. They automatically use their age and supportive parents to reach their objective to obtain funds regardless how insignificant it seems for the project desired. Most of these females' prime objective is to be beautiful in the sense of how good and appealing they look in the eyes of others. This is an area wherein they lose their sense of value pertaining to economics, succumbing to expensive hair preparations, toenails and hand nails (manicure, polished and designed), tattoos, exclusive wearing apparel, expensive jewelry, high-priced shoes, and food purchasing (usually fast foods establishments).

Their awareness of reaching the status of puberty has shown in recent years they have very little regards for the responsibility of that stage of their lives to avoid numerous pitfalls of consequences. Even though parents, along with numerous teachers, inform many female youth, nevertheless the youth assume it will not affect their lifestyle pertaining to their offspring(s) or abortion.

As the saying goes, "babies having babies" at an alarming rate create tremendous social problems and issues that they do not have the matured mental capabilities nor the experiences to cope with in nurturing their offspring(s).

Secondly, certain known and suspected unknown diseases are so prevalent. Scientists indeed are baffled as to their control or eradication even with prescribed pharmaceutical drugs. However, researchers are constantly putting forth tireless efforts searching for cures and, most of all, informing society of preventive measures to combat these dreaded diseases.

The majority of female youth, along with their male counterparts, often lack discernment pertaining to sexual activities. They assume that they will not be infected regardless of how often or what methods are involved, omitting the fact that the probability of acquiring sexual transmitted diseases (STD or HIV-AIDS) is indeed possible regardless of how carefully you performed.

There is hope and a solution to avoid these devastating factors mentioned heretofore simply with sincere, concern and care with absolute discernment and prayer to Jehovah God.

The Apopka Chief, August 26, 2011, Page 11A

Cleaning Edgewood Colored Cemetery part of Labor Day memories

The Labor Day holiday relative to America was conceived during the 19th century from our neighbors the Canadians who, for years, had adopted labor laws and regulations pertaining to Labor Day festivities. This holiday was partially approved and recognized by only a few states as a federal holiday in 1894. However, in 2009 the entire 50 states finally complied.

As a boy, Slim and the neighborhood crew would cherish the thought of Labor Day festivities on the first Monday in September very shortly after the dog days of August.

In Apopka's ghetto population, since the second decade of the 20th century, citizens of that area have religiously cleaned a designated area of Edgewood Colored Cemetery once per year on Labor Day.

However, at that point in time, the city of Apopka had not officially agreed relative to the responsibility of administrating and maintenance of that portion of the cemetery until the 1970s. During the 1920s, a group of Apopka Negro businesses, along with Mrs. Martha A. Board, a prominent citizen, organized a committee to oversee caretaking and management of Apopka's Edgewood Colored Cemetery until records and monies were turned over and agreed upon that the city of Apopka was to become stewards of in the 1970.

80 Apopka Colored Cemetery now known as part of Edgewood-Greenwood Cemetery. Photo by DrO 2015

Previously, Slim mentioned how we youngsters anticipated the food and that lemonade "old man" made. Most adults relished the meeting of friends after a year of absence and a sense of dignity for the deceased by maintaining the area. Tom Barnes, a committee member, was assigned year after year to prepare two wooden 55-gallon barrels of lemonade. Allen Prince Chisholm was delegated to supply many pounds of mullet fish for frying. Bill Chandler was to obtain equipment or tools necessary for landscaping.

Arthur Willis was labor coordinator expeditor. Mrs. Hannah Williams was overseer of food preparation. A local grove service, Gilliam & Goding, provided equipment and tools, and Michael Gladden was chief organizer of activities.

This cleanup project, from its initiation in the 1920s, stemmed from the fact that Apopka Negro Businesses Organization did not have necessary monetary funds to employ personnel to maintain the cemetery on a regular basis, therefore, the idea of community participation was conceived and continued for at least four decades.

Many old timers of that era often remind Slim of what a community can accomplish regardless of the hardships. Also, they extend their sincere thanks to persons for three or four decades of involvement and vision. Memories of that past era relative to Labor Day activities will be etched forever in participants' minds of the anticipation and enjoyment.

The Pennings of Perrine Slim

The Apopka Chief, September 2, 2011, Page 12A

Railroad upgrade would help Apopka economy

In Apopka in the 1880's, when railroading began to become a prevalent form of transporting people and goods, this accelerated the growth of new towns that eventually became established cities. Railroads definitely played a significant role in building America, then and to some extent even now. Several rail proposals warrant completion to continue building the American trend.

Presently, in the 21st century, Lake-Orange County district where the TO&A Railroad tracks system runs, there is a proposal regarding construction pertaining to vast improvement of the existing aged railroad tracks in order to safely increase flow of rail traffic wherein to attract manufacturers of light industries, businesses, and tourists.

These tracks can date back to the 19th Century when TO&A Railroad Company (SAL) conceived the idea of building a railroad through Apopka. This proposal was offered with the slight objection of a few landowners of the proposed route, thus precipitating change of the original surveyed route and delaying the agreed time schedule of completion.

At that time, shortly after the TO&A finalized track construction, the Midland Railroad Company

(ACL) was the second railroad company to construct tracks and established its station depot at U.S. 441 and Forest Avenue slightly north of the rail junction. Both of these railroad companies provided adequate freight and passenger services twice per day well into the 1950's. However, Midland's (ACL) passenger service declined rapidly in the Apopka area precipitated by the Clarcona-Apopka transfer connection. Nevertheless, Midland (ACL) operated solely on the basis of a freight carrier until terminating its business in Apopka and removing its entire railroad system (tracks, station-depot, gates, switches, and crossing signs) from Apopka.

Within the Apopka railroad district from 1920-1950, from Lockhart to the Lake County line, the TO&A employed a local section crew for track maintenance with a storage shop behind Apopka's ice plant on South Central Avenue adjacent to the TO&A mainline railroad tracks. This shop housed the railroad handcars, tools, railroad tracks and track parts.

Slim was very familiar with the entire section crew personnel and their job description beginning with crew foreman Turk; Sam Briar, lead section hand, Old man "Big" Smith; Birthel Simpkins; Moses Howard; F. M. Slade, handcar operator; Joe Martin; Ernest Walker; Wilfred A. Sanders, flagman and torpedo specialist; Dowell Briar; Bishop George Washington, and John Gant.

Midland Railroad's (ACL) storage areas, track maintenance shop and section crew's family quarters were in Clarcona at the rail split for the Ocoee and Winter Garden-Oakland routes. WWII accelerated numerous changes in track construction and the purchasing of additional right of ways. Each of the railroad companies adapted to upholding their commitment as railroad carriers pertaining to transporting war supplies and troops relative to the war efforts.

Slim recalls during that era (1941-1946) TO&A recruited several professional railroad "extra gang" workers who resided on TO&A then accommodating railroad cars with sleeping quarters, galley, hygiene facilities, storage-shop maintenance car, commissary and lounge area.

Usually these special cars were placed on the sidetracks of the mainline for unlimited time wherein they were convenient for "extra gang" personnel when repairing and installing track from Mount Dora through Apopka to Fairvilla. Due to the Midland Railroad's (ACL) section crew division at the Clarcona split locale, that rail route had very limited war plants or factories relative to the war efforts, therefore it stands to reason why very little improvement or rail construction was done stemming from lack of rail traffic through its system.

Though present day proposals for rail improvement on the existing TO&A Railroad between the Lake County Line and Orlando have met considerable opposition for areas through Apopka, this area stands to benefit substantially, provided the area officials of Apopka, namely the Apopka Area Chamber of Commerce are in agreement with the proposals.

The Chamber has put forth tireless efforts into recruiting light factory, industries, tourist attractions such as Lake Apopka-Zellwood Farm Lands, Zellwood famous mansions, Rock Springs (run, caverns) and businesses to relocate in close proximity to the tracks in the area locales.

Presently, along the TO&A Railroad tracks' right-of-way in Apopka, there exists many acres of accessible property feasible for establishing light industrial factories or businesses wherein convenience and locale would satisfy all parties involved and possibly bring some rail transport business back into the area.

The Apopka Chief, September 9, 2011, Page 13A

Salvaging for a livelihood puts damper on litter

Aluminum Can Salvage Endeavors, Salvaging for a Livelihood, Reducing Littering.

Since Slim was a boy more than 75 years ago, containers for the purposes of holding liquids, especially for human consumption, have changed drastically. The advent of these various containers for holding both edible solids and liquids has taken many shapes and forms and content. To promote the present day era of recycling and technological advancement of resources, within mother's nature realm, enhances the longevity arena of conservation.

Many decades ago, most liquids for human consumption were contained in glass containers. However, since that period, due to scientific exploration, several other materials –namely plastics and aluminum – have come to the point where they are utilized extensively for containment.Even beverages some 25 years ago, especially soda water, were contained in returnable-deposit glass bottles that held different liquid equivalent ounces. This was the container of choice.

Even then, the trend for salvaging was apparent

and orchestrated a monetary deposit for the container when the item was purchased. This deposit was then returned for financial refund when the container was returned to a store or other establishment that sold these products. Eventually, these bottles were returned to ownership firms (bottlers) wherein they were thoroughly sanitized and reused accordingly.

Linda Scott Poole was one of the renowned female salvage engineers on a consistent basis in the immediate area of Apopka. She is often considered as a dedicated aluminum can salvage engineer; mother, grandmother and a neighbor of Slim's for at least a decade. She has been specializing in salvaging, especially aluminum cans and other salvageable products for many years.

On a daily basis, Ms. Poole's endeavors initiate at approximately 6 a.m. from her home site. She prepares her four-wheeled cart with needed equipment: radio, cell telephone, foul weather gear, rubber gloves, grapple apparatus, and filled drinking water bottles. (Ms. Poole finds all this equipment to be portions of the equation for the three-mile trek that she ventures on when salvaging.) Ms. Poole finds many items on her route, especially aluminum cans and other salvageable products along the roadside, in front of neighbors' homes and numerous businesses.

These salvageable products are placed within the

cart. Usually, this three-mile trek of walking and pushing the cart entails approximately five hours per day, four days per week. Periodically, she does business transactions with a local salvage recycling company relative to aluminum cans accumulated for monetary gains pertaining to poundage presented.

Many citizens are very appreciative of Ms. Linda Poole's endeavors relative to picking up stored cans from their household dwelling and last, but not least, somewhat placing a damper on littering. Along with this, Ms. Poole is able to keep active, get much air and exercise, and communicate with the various neighbors that she encounters as she walks.

Thanks, Ms. Poole!

81 Gladden's Store on now Michael Gladden Blvd at Central Ave.
Photo from F. Boykin.

Achievements of pioneer negroes beneficial to society

Regardless of Difficulties--A prelude to this article titled "Prelude To Achievers" was about the many educators in Orange County who influenced many of our present-day achievers.

Previously in the early penning of *The Apopka Chief* column Bits 'n' Tips by Ms. Mildred A. Board, there were several articles pertaining to achievements of Negroes who were nurtured in the Northwest Orange County area (Tangerine, Zellwood, Plymouth, Clarcona, and Apopka). These articles heightened concern whenever comparing persons of present-day achievements.

82 Mildred A. Board, Educator. Boykin

Recently, Slim has been constantly reminded through one-on-one conversation and group meetings that the achievements of the era of the late

20th century should be noted occasionally in the column. Those achievements, especially of the younger generation's input to society, should be identified.

Hopefully, in future writing, it will not be intentional to omit anyone who Slim is aware of or informed about through reliable resources. Please take into consideration that, over many decades, hundreds of accomplishments have been ascertained; therefore, it will limit names noted.

Numerous pioneer individuals of the Northwest Orange County area, without a doubt, should be noted for their contribution role of achieving in the late 19th century and early 20th century, namely Sarah Mead, entrepreneur; Daniel M. Giddens, stone mason; Steven Hooper, railroad worker, landowner and real estate salesman; George Oden, citrus farmer; Sam Small Sr., preacher, NAACP coordinator and vegetable farmer; Ella Walls, rental entrepreneur; Henry Terrell, blacksmith; Michael Gladden Sr., grocery merchant; Jules Vann, citrus grower, landowner; Daniel Butler, special sand stone mason; Herman M. Mobley, grocery store entrepreneur; and Olivia Pierce, school teacher.

Heretofore mentioned individuals of Slim's heritage, according to documentation, had very little or no formal academic training. However, this did not hinder their thirst for pursuing achievement in numerous arenas that were beneficial to society.

Those pioneer individuals' leadership roles were key factors in orchestrating today's achievers, including James Davis, homegrown, academia Orange County Public Schools, Florida A&M University, accredited electrical teacher, politics, FAMU lobbyist; Douglas Sanders, nurtured in Apopka, secondary education OCPS, University of Florida medical school, the first of his ethnicity and upbringing in Apopka to become a physician; Dickey Parker, reared in Apopka, attended OCPS, FAMU graduate, prominent agriculture teacher for OCPS, Masonic affiliation high levels; Willie Webb Jr., Apopka born, OCPS graduate, U.S. military, maintenance entrepreneur, neighborhood mentor for teenagers; Robert Willis Jr., OCPS, entrepreneur, former city of Apopka maintenance department lead person; Rossie Thomas Bellamy, professional nurse, OCPS graduate, attended Grady School of Nursing (Atlanta, Georgia), first certified nurse when Apopka Farm Workers Health Clinic was established; Augustine Jackson Dudley, reared in Tangerine, OCPS, talented athlete, OCPS graduate, FAMU degree, OCPS teacher, outstanding public speaker; and Moses Payne, born in Alabama, raised in Apopka, graduated OCPS, earned a degree at Tuskegee Institute, ROTC officer, retired full colonel of the U.S. Army.

These are just a few of the individuals whose accomplishments are well known to Slim and others in the locality as people who were reared in the surrounding area and have gone away from the Central Florida area to gain other educational or vocational skills and have migrated back to utilize those skills gainfully. The attitude of getting an education or vocation was inculcated into them from a very early age and they did this very well.

Thanks to all of you who took the education that you were given by the early pioneers of Orange County education and made the best of it by bringing back and motivating others to follow in your footsteps.

83 The Lodge as originally built in 1859. AHS

The Pennings of Perrine Slim

The Apopka Chief, September 30, 2011, Page 11A

Negro pioneers contributed much to communities

Initial History of Area Negro Achievers

Slim is very fortunate to have known the majority of individuals that he writes about whether they are Caucasians or Negroes. This personal knowledge, along with having documented information and reputable concrete sources of information, makes his information very valuable. It is a known fact it is necessary to have all ethnic groups involved in society's gains and successes.

In and around the 1840s-1850s, according to records, the majority of Negroes in our area not living with the Seminole Indian tribes as free persons in Northwest Orange County were enslaved by several prominent Caucasian farmers, two of whom were William S. Delk and William C. Goolsby. There were a few other slave owners in the Rock Springs-Sorrento area before the 1861-1865 War between the States at that point in time and it was a means of survival for all parties involved.

The mass early arrival of Negroes came in Northwest Orange County due to the abolishment of slavery initiated shortly after the conclusion of the War Between the States in 1865, which was also known as the period of Reconstruction in America.

There were numerous tributaries and entryways leading to the St. Johns River, namely Ocklawaha River, Rock Springs Run, Wekiva River, and Clay Springs. These were all available means of waterway travel for the Apopka area because it was more accommodating for their needs when on the move and less expensive.

These early Negro settlers mostly migrated from the states of Georgia, South Carolina, North Carolina, and Alabama. However, during the 1880s, the railroad industry initiated massive construction throughout Florida, the turpentine industry blossomed, and citrus farming was on the rise. Therefore, these early settlers were given the incentive to seek gainful employment, adventure, homes, entrepreneurship, sharecropping, and lands for farming.

Persons of color have indeed made numerous immeasurable contributions to our petite communities of Zellwood, Clarcona, Tangerine, Plymouth, and Rock Springs-Sorrento during the 19th century into the 21st century. Both genders along with then two Negro churches (New Hope Missionary Baptist Church and St. Paul AME Church) were very influential in these early Negro settlers' lives pertaining to morals, principles, academia, sharecropping, and entrepreneurship.

84 **New Hope Missionary Baptist Church and Congregation on 04 June 1901. Photo from Orange County Regional History Center.**

The nucleus locale of these early Negro families in the 1880s was in the immediate area of "The Lodge," which was constructed in 1859, and consisted of families such as the Giddens, Kent, Darby, Mitchell, Rand, Girtman, Logan, Weaver, Pickett, Mead, Rainey, Chisholm, and Oden, and several others not intentionally omitted. According to reputable social scientists and certain governmental agencies, three of these early Negro settlers (Mead, Hooper, and Oden) were indeed superb achievers relative to their endeavors and community initiating in the latter 19th century and continuous until the third decade of the 20th century.

85 Stephen Hooper family property tax receipt March 30, 1876. Photo of original doc by DrO 2015

In and around the second decade of the 1900s, appeared several individuals (Mobley, Gladden, Terrell, Sanders, and Hayward) of the same ethnicity as the early Negro settlers and began achieving status as society's achievers. Simuel Burrell, favorably called "Bubbie," was born and nurtured in Apopka prior to WWII. Mr. Burrell obtained his primary and secondary education within OCPS. He attended a major northeastern shoe manufacturing company for shoe repair, etc. During his upbringing, Bubbie always affiliated himself in and around some form of established businesses relative to grocery merchandise and shoe repairing.

This association was indeed the catalyst that precipitated his desire to become an entrepreneur while living in New York during the 1960s-1970s. Returning to Florida in the 1970s, Bubbie pursued several avenues relative to merchandising articles. While living in Orlando, he ventured into promoting shoe shining at six downtown business locales. His previous experiences pertaining to shoe care and repair precipitated his establishing ownership of three modern shoe repair shops in that area. Along with his daughter, they opened an exclusive shoe store in the downtown Orlando business district.

Also, around the turn of the 20th century, his involvement in religion became pronounced, thus encouraging him to seek studying and becoming ordained in theology at Freedom Ministries in Apopka under the watchful scrutiny of the renowned pastor Freddie Fillmore Sr. Presently, as an ordained minister, he has religious programs at area jail facilities every week.

Simuel Burrell credits his business procedures and practices sanctioned by Jehovah God along with constant nudging acquired from his father (John Burrell Sr.) and two Negro businessmen (Gladden brothers) in Apopka. Last but not least, without a doubt, numerous soul sisters and soul brothers are wearing foot apparel that Bubbie repaired or donated (smile).

86 Doctor Thomas Eliot "Doc Tommy" McBride Road, Designated by: 2010 Legislature of Florida. Photo Dr.O. 2012 12 29

Clark's Corner mill site was the focal point of the community

Pioneer Family Names Are Still Existing

Clark's Corner (aka Clarcona), a petite community approximately three miles south of Apopka, came into existence shortly after the Florida Seminole Indian Wars of the late 1840s. Clark's Corner was inhabited mostly by people who herded livestock and farmed.

William Clark, a businessman for whom the town of Clarcona was named, was a native from the state of Connecticut. In and around 1886, Clark purchased several hundred acres of land in the Lakeville and Clarcona area laden with longleaf pine trees wherein to establish a prominent sawmill to compete with Consumers Lumber & Veneer Company of Apopka and to coexist with the nearby turpentine industry at that point in time that was the chief source of income. Clark's Corner mill site became the focal point of that area and was enhanced by the Orange Belt Railroad, which constructed tracks from Lake Monroe to Oakland, passing through Clark's Corner mill site. Railroading orchestrated the ideal means at that point in time of transporting commodities, passengers, and U.S. mail.

The once-prominent sawmilling site is non-existent, along with the numerous turpentine distillers that were once in abundance. However, portions of the original rail system tracks are being used daily to service the cities of Ocoee and Winter Garden. The northern track system leaving Clarcona via Fuller's Crossing into Winter Garden nowadays has been converted from rails into an upscale well-traveled bike trail.

Some of the offspring of the early pioneer families ancestry still reside in area, maintaining their families' heritages. These are families like Gilliam, Kellogg, Cumbie, Marden, Fawcett, Walker, Fuller, Cogswell, Session, Williams, Whitfield, Wallace, and Clark.

Clark's Corner never had an abundance of businesses heretofore, as most commerce was mainly a general store, sawmilling, turpentine distilling, blacksmith shop, and post office. Some of these have relocated or are out of business.

Mr. Garrett Gilliam's grandfather was a postmaster. The Gilliam family gained notoriety in their achievements relative to being superb game hunters and citrus groves caretakers. Nowadays, most of the massive citrus groves and an abundance of forest areas have been replaced with housing development on an enormous scale. Horseshoe Lake, in that date and time, was the recreational center for those families.

87 Leroy W. Gilliam, Postmaster of the Clarcona Post Office 1 March 1909-17 December 1916. Notice the cancellation stamps showing through the paper. Photo from Belle Gilliam.

The Midland Railroad water tower, depot, mail catching apparatus, section handwork shop, and housing quarters for section crews' families all have been demolished.

© 2015

There was also an OCPS elementary classroom facility on the east side of County 435/Apopka-Vineland Road and Clarcona-Ocoee Road [south of the railroad track] that served both races [over different periods of time] relative to public education in the area and, at one point in time, was moved to Apopka Junior High School in approximately 1950.

Another interesting fact of the area is that the Whitfield and Fawcett grove service living quarters have made way for housing development. CR 435 initiating from its focal point in Clarcona through Apopka to Rock Springs has had a name change. Through the persistence of Florida Legislators Fredrick Brummer and Bryan Nelson, wherein to honor longtime prominent physician of Northwest Orange County, Thomas E. McBride, M.D., the name of the road was officially changed to honor Dr. McBride.

The Apopka Chief, October 14, 2011, Page 13A

Citizens should share responsibility to reduce crime rates

Assuming Pride and Concern

Because of the most frustrating crimes that are occurring on a daily basis, it is necessary that as of "rat now" we, as law-abiding citizens, share some of the responsibility along with current Orange County Sheriff Jerry Demings and his deputies in order to slow the crime statistics to a level that is considerably lower.

Ninety-five percent of our crime issues stem from within our own dominion and we have become complacent in relying completely on law-enforcement officials to solve all of our problems without our help. In order to affect this statistic and aid in solving some of our problems or deterring people from being involved in these crimes, we badly need a civilian police patrol.

Several years ago, in 2003, the Orange County Sheriff's Department was given a grant to establish a civilian police patrol for the area below the TO&A Railroad tracks in order to assist the sheriff's office in crime prevention, emergency medical treatment, and rescue operations. Due to the fact that the areas the sheriff's officers cover are so large, it limits their presence on a daily basis. Therefore, it is necessary that a civilian police patrol be incorporated, wherein they can be the eyes and ears for deputies who are not present during the occurrence of many of these incidents.

A large doublewide office trailer was placed on the OCPS properties at South Central Avenue and 18th Street in Apopka as the base of operations for the proposed program heretofore mentioned. At that point in time, Deputy Rick Wisecup was assigned to direct this program along with Deputy Danny Anderson.

They advised numerous pastors in the community that they were actively attempting to get this program established and organized for the area below the TO&A Railroad tracks. A meeting was scheduled and held at John H. Bridges Community Center with numerous elite ranking sheriffs' office officials in attendance who work in the area on a daily basis. But, for lack of interest among community citizens as to what this program brings to our area, attendance was extremely low.

Deputy Wisecup made an excellent presentation relative to how the program would be established and its benefits for the area below the TO&A Railroad tracks. Deputies Wisecup and Anderson plan to schedule a meeting next spring and, hopefully, there will be at least 30-40 men and women who are 21 years or older in order to jumpstart this program.

Citizens of this area, "let's wake up" and assume interest in our community. The officials need our help tremendously. It has to be a community effort. Let's get sincere and responsible about how and where we live. Don't let "Junior and Sally Mae" forget that we have strict principles and morals that are necessary in order for these hideous acts of crime and violence to not be tolerated.

Under no circumstances should these things be allowed and we have to think of the Bible where it states that there is a price – an eye for an eye – for the performance of acts that go against God's statutes and man's law and this price must be paid in order for these abnormal acts to be discontinued.

Within the past year, Orange County has crime levels compared to what New Orleans experienced after Hurricane Katrina. It is time that we as mature adults put forth massive efforts to curtail some of the most frustrating crimes that are occurring on a daily basis. It is necessary that, as of NOW, we as citizens share some of being responsible, along with Sheriff Jerry Demings and his deputies, in order to slow down these crime statistics.

Again, 95 percent of our crime issues stem from within our own neighborhood and in our own household dwellings, but we have a tendency to look the other way while praying and pleading that law-enforcement officials completely resolve the problem. Then, when they do try to solve the problem (i.e. drug stings, prostitution, etc.), we find ourselves complaining on television about how some criminal's' rights were violated. Wake up. Only we can take our neighborhood back, it should not have to be up to the sheriff to come in and run the criminals out of town. This is why the civilian police patrol needs to be established for our community.

Early Negro settlers contributed much to the Northwest Orange County area

Individuals and Innovations

Northwest Orange County indeed should give numerous cheers of thanks to the efforts, dedications, concerns and visions to a few individuals who strived to ascertain economic stability. William S. Delk, a native from the state of Georgia, arrived in Florida shortly after the Seminole Indian Wars in Florida in the late 1840s, seeking prominence as an entrepreneur and farmer in this abundant virgin forest area of tree varieties and waterways in the Rock Springs area.

Delk homesteaded hundreds of acres of longleaf pine trees for harvesting (turpentine or lumber), multiple acres for farming in addition to controlling Rock Springs Run and Rock Springs which Delk's innovations precipitated that source of water kinetic energy to propel his sawmilling apparatus and grinding mill machinery equipment enterprises. During portions of the U.S. Civil War, Delk was forced to abandon the area, but returned immediately after the conclusion of the war wherein to reclaim his properties and resume his businesses and farming. Delk's demise occurred in the 1880s and his widow sold the properties to Thomas E. Wilson.

Shortly after the Civil War, Steven Hooper, a person of color, was employed by the railroad construction industry (extra gang) during their massive building of railroads throughout Central Florida, especially in the Apopka area, wherein he purchased and sold acres of valuable properties. Hooper eventually homesteaded a parcel of land in the Rock Springs area.

His son, Lawrence, became sole heir of Hooper's properties after his demise at the Rock Spring area. According to documentation, the Steven Hooper family at that point in time owned more property than any other Negro family in the Apopka area.

Sarah Mead was of Negro ethnicity born into slavehood in approximately 1835 in the state of South Carolina and was sold at a very young age (12 years) to a plantation owner in the state of Georgia where she remained until the conclusion of the Civil War in 1865. While enslaved in Georgia, she met and married Lindsly Mead in 1857 of the same heritage.

Before departing Georgia several years after the war, Sarah and Lindsly Mead initiated an entrepreneurship relative to affordable housing rentals and commissary to accommodate many ex-slaves.

Through networking during a brief period of the U.S. Reconstruction days, Sarah contacted her sister who lived in Jacksonville who advised Sarah of the potential of families exploring Florida for their livelihood. This mass migration precipitated the Meads to relocate in Apopka and homestead wherein to establish and continue their heretoforementioned entrepreneurship.

George Oden of Negro heritage born in the state of Alabama near Talladega ventured into Northwest Orange County approximately in and around the eighth decade of the 19th century, pursuing his dreams of farming relative to his native Alabama. However, citrus being on the rise at that time precipitated Oden's agriculture endeavors towards citrus caretaking and eventually ownership of a 40-acre bearing citrus grove near Marshall Lake chain of lakes in Apopka. George Oden donated the property he purchased in 1894 adjacent to his homestead in Apopka to the present-day New Hope Missionary Baptist Church locale.

Amos Starbird, who was nurtured in a northeastern state (Maine) of the good ole U.S.A. during the 19th century, was advised of the abundance lumbering endeavors in Florida. In and around the 1880s, Amos moved to Orlando seeking exploration of the timber industry in Northwest Orange County. At this point in time, several petite sawmills were for sale in the Apopka area that he and his sons purchased. CL&VC mill became the chief employer in the Apopka area in addition to manufacturing wood containers. The

Starbird family's innovations relative to technology pertaining to furnishing fresh water supply and electricity was indeed an advancement into the 20th century for the community.

John T. Pirie, a prominent businessman (dry goods) in Chicago, Illinois, from Lake Forest, Illinois, began (1892) staying his winter months in Central Florida at nearby Plymouth. Pirie, after his first visits in 1892, spent the next 48 years staying only during the winter months relative to wild game hunting, land conservation, citrus production, and animal husbandry. Shortly after 1892, through his visions and efforts, John Pirie's holdings in Florida had peaked to the stage where they needed constant overseeing. Observing William Edwards, a Scotsman affiliated with the Chicago YMCA, as to his expertise of organization, Pirie, without hesitation, employed Edwards to manage the entire Florida Pirie holding. Edwards should be highly credited with the success achieved at the Pirie estate and other Northwest Orange County Estates in Zellwood during his tenure. William Edwards' influence and persistence in 1912 orchestrated the establishing of the State Bank of Apopka in addition to management and growth of Plymouth Citrus Growers Exchange for a period of 20 years. In 1921, Edwards, while at PCGE, obtained an electric generating plant capable of supplying electric energy for Plymouth into Zellwood on a 24-hour daily demand as mandated.

Richard Whitney was from the state of New York and was a prominent financer and president of New York Stock Exchange for five terms. He arrived in the area in and around the 1890s pursing several business opportunities, land acquisition, and wild game hunting. At one point in time (1930), Richard Whitney purchased stock in the State Bank of Apopka. In its infancy, during the Great Depression, Whitney became the chief stockholder and vice president.

In the second decade of the 1900s, Richard Whitney established and owned Stauffer Chemical Company in Apopka relative to insecticide production. He also owned 30,000 acres of wild game hunting preserves in and around Mount Plymouth.

88 Lula Davis served the Edwards family for 45 years. Called Mammy, she died in 1946. AHS

Bus was only reliable transportation in old days

Slim recalls back in the early 1940s when the Orlando Transit Company (OTC), a privately owned business was the only local bus commuter carrier for Northwest Orange County out of Apopka (to and fro) from Zellwood, Plymouth, Lockhart, and Orlando. These trips occurred four times per day initiating with two trips in the morning before noon and two afternoon trips before 6 p.m. The entire existence of OTC as a transit enterprise during this period (1940s-1950s) its policies and procedures adhered to the times pertaining to Jim Crow laws (1875-1965) with few incidents.

During the 1940s era, that was mentioned, very few families had the convenience of personal transportation capable of making trips to Orlando without mechanical or financial difficulty. Therefore, this initiated the availability and convenience of the OTC commuter transit system with destinations relative to Apopka-Orlando was well received and used exclusively for courthouse appearances, business transactions, sporting events, Central Florida fairgrounds, and department store shopping, especially on Thursday, Friday, and Saturday. OTC at that time did not operate their system on Sundays. Also, Negro

© 2015

secondary academia students from Northwest Orange County area, at that point in time (1945-1947), had only one public high school in the entire county located in Orlando for their heritage and no means of OCPS-owned buses.

However, at this point in time, the schools and OTC agreed to subsidize commuter fares (offering a 50-cents-per-week booklet) for public school students commuting on the OTC system.

After a period of time, OCPS would eventually expedite creating transporting students with their own OCPS bus system. In and around the latter part of the fourth decade into the fifth decade, OTC terminated their commuter services in the Apopka area.

In approximately 1980, the Lynx transit system sanctioned by the Orange County Commission concurred to create a transit route from Apopka to Orlando. At that point in time, Rufus "Chicken George" Gilmore, who was employed at Lynx as one of their trusted and premier drivers, was asked about the probability of an Apopka route.

Being that Rufus Gilmore was nurtured and received secondary education in Apopka therefore, without hesitation or doubt relative to Gilmore having the expertise and knowledge of the area, Lynx delegated him the task of thoroughly researching and submitting a feasible commuter bus route and schedule for Apopka-Orlando area. Gilmore spent numerous hours studying the proposed bus route and surveying the area while driving throughout the entire populated sector below the TO&A Railroad tracks into Clarcona on a daily basis for several weeks. This was done prior to a final approved route while promoting the commuter service for the area in addition to consulting with the city, Orange County commissioners, Florida state officials and potential patrons as to their input of a feasible bus route and scheduling.

Eventually, the first designated route entailed bus stops continuously every two blocks from U.S. Highway 441 and South Park Avenue, along Park Avenue to East Cleveland Street, to South Central Avenue, then back to U.S. 441 and North Central Avenue.

The scheduling was adopted wherein to accommodate those patrons who had early or evening job appointments in addition to buses running every hour on the hour daily (exception of Sunday) from 5 a.m. until 10 p.m.

At this point in time, only one route was available to and fro, namely bus 41. Currently, there are four routes into the Apopka area (17, 41, 44, 405) that enable riders to reach destinations directly or transferring in order to reach destinations in one of the three immediate surrounding counties, Lake, Seminole, and Osceola.

We citizens and patrons of Lynx system wholeheartedly commend and thank Rufus Gilmore for his concerns, vision and dedication wherein to benefit mankind. Thank you, "Chicken George!" (Smile.)

The Apopka Chief, November 11, 2011, Page 13A

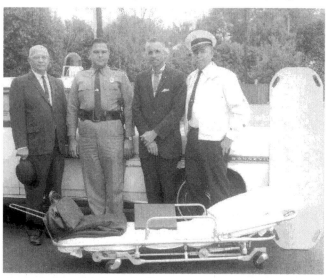

89 Unkown, Police Chief John Holloway, Fire Chief Leroy Gilliam and Mayor John H. Land. This photo accompanied original article. AFD

Fire Chief Leroy Gilliam remembered for wisdom, concern and contributions

Chief of Fire Chiefs

This penning was precipitated through the admiration and respect that Slim has for the late Leroy Gilliam, the city of Apopka fire chief for many years. Regardless of the environment or city in this good old U.S.A., Fire Chief Gilliam ranked with the best or better, according to Slim's eyewitness incidents in the major U.S. cities of Miami, Atlanta, New York City, San Francisco, and San Diego.

In October 2011, a 21st century owner of a 19th-century wooden structure dwelling requested of the

Apopka Fire Department to monitor, for the purpose of practicing fire-burning control, the controlled burning of a wooden constructed frame house built in the 1890s and owned then by Daniel Butler at 28 East Michael Gladden Blvd, Apopka. This unusual event reminded Slim of numerous situations when the illustrious Fire Chief of Chiefs Leroy Gilliam was at the helm orchestrating and supervising the firefighting personnel.

Leroy "Roy" Gilliam was nurtured in portions of Orange County and Clarcona. His prestigious family was very instrumental in the exiguous town of Clarcona. His fraternal grandfather was one of the original postmasters for the local area.

90 Arlie Franklin Gilliam, father of Roy and Garrett Gilliam. AHS

Roy's father, Arlie Gilliam, was a prominent citrus caretaker, Orange County School Board trustee, and proven wild game hunter.

Roy served in the U.S. Navy in WWII before returning to Orlando to initiate his firefighting career with a "full steam-ahead" attitude. Roy left the firefighting arena for a period of time when he ventured into the citrus caretaking business that was previously owned by his father, and Roy's brother, Garrett Gilliam.

Mayor John H. Land of Apopka recruited Leroy Gilliam for the position of fire chief in the city of Apopka. At that time, Apopka had only one fire truck that was manned only by volunteer firefighters who were local entrepreneurs, like Roy himself. Once the city's siren wailed, those volunteers would rush from their businesses to the old City Hall that housed the fire truck and make preparations to proceed to the fire scene.

Due to his caretaking enterprises, many times Chief Gilliam would be contacted via his truck telephone to respond to a call.

You would occasionally see and hear the chief rushing along the streets in his personally owned red pickup truck with his emergency lights flashing and siren wailing to respond to the emergency.

Over the years, Chief Roy observed the fire department with great concern, passion and vision beyond his time well into the 21st century pertaining to equipment, personnel, building codes and technology that even today's Apopka modern departments adhere to his experiences and guidelines.

In the early 1960s, under the tutelage of Chief Gilliam, a group of Negro men in the Apopka area (TO&A Railroad) was trained in safety measures, accident procedures, and emergency medical treatment. The training received by most of the firefighters under Chief Roy's control was considered immeasurable.

Chief Leroy Gilliam was favorably called "Roy" by all who knew him. My personal involvement with Roy stemmed from firefighting, citrus, agriculture, and emergency medical treatment.

His vision on projected population growth and what infrastructure would be needed to support it was amazing. His visual blueprint that he so vividly described for the areas of Rock Springs, Plymouth, Apopka (TO.&A), Binion Road, Clarcona, and Lake Apopka is being partially addressed today without reservations by those localities.

I recall a program he discussed with me at length that he initiated concerning the old fire district at Clarcona, Apopka (TO&A Railroad), and Lake

Apopka, and was later voted down to his dismay. At that time, the city of Apopka was responsible for the coverage of those areas. After several years of legal wrangling, Orange County assumed the responsibility of providing fire coverage for the previously mentioned areas. Orange County stations 28 and 40 have done a superb job of fire protection coverage due to his expertise, vision, and dedication to that area. Very few cities or counties have their own fire training facilities. However, through his vision, the city of Apopka built one such facility prior to his retirement and honored him by dedicating the facility in his name. Several cities and counties throughout the state utilize it for training purposes.

Although Roy's demise occurred several years ago, most local citizens who knew him still miss him tremendously for his wisdom, concern, and contributions. Chief Leroy "Roy" Gilliam, we all thank you for your contributions for our safety and wellbeing. Also noteworthy in mentioning that even at his age, when he was the chief, Roy could and would participate in all phases of activities that modern, young firefighters were responsible for (fires, accident scenes, medical assistance, and water rescue).

91 Fire Chief Leroy Gilliam commanding at a fire scene. AFD

Remember sacrifices, struggles of foreparents for education–determine to achieve

Society Urban Progress Created Tremendous Changes

As of the 21st century, there should not be any plausible reason for individuals to not obtain complete academia certification in our public school system beyond the eighth grade.

Nowadays, in 2011, the majority of individuals who are primary and secondary education students are quitting school thus not fully completing the basic required academia in order to compete in the system of things.

If only these wayward students were to apply some discernment relative to from whence we have come wherein to ascertain a complete secondary education, their reasoning should and will have positive tendencies pertaining to acquiring a competent education.

Within Orange County, certain northwest rural areas consisting of a small Negro population initiating in the late 19th century into the 20th century (1947) that education for Negroes remained at the primary educational phase ONLY. These educational programs offered pupils the equivalent of an eighth grade education due to the fact there was only one public heritage high school (Jones High) accessible in the entire Orange County Public School System at that point in time for persons of color to complete secondary education. Once students of this ethnicity ascertained that plateau of primary academia (eighth grade), the majority of families could not financially afford commuter fees nor board their student in Orlando. Nevertheless, there was one heritage private high school (Hungerford) in Orange County.

However, it strictly required from parents all financial support for student's board, room, and tuition fees for the final four years of secondary education. If by some ways and means, a student was awarded a financial scholarship, this was acceptable at Hungerford. Of the pupils of the aforementioned heritage residing in those rural Orange County Public Schools areas at that point in time who completed the primary phase of academia, 99 percent of them were immediately thrust into the workforce doing common labor.

Finally, through legislation, it was absolutely necessary to adopt, pass, and enforce the children's labor laws wherein students of those rural areas and color were not forced into labor situations due to Orange County Public Schools not having a secondary education phase for pupils of those rural sectors.

Hungerford High School negotiated an educational agreement in 1947 relative to secondary education with OCPS to accept public school students of colored heritage from the northwest sections of Orange County in addition to Maitland, Forest City, and Winter Park at Hungerford in Eatonville, this alleviated numerous issues at that point in time pertaining to integration, school bus transportation, building new high school facilities, and continuation of academia beyond the eighth grade.

In addition, Orange County Public Schools administrative officials would develop and be responsible for a school bus transporting system initiating in approximately 1947 for pupils of color out of the rural areas of Northwest Orange County, including several areas heretofore mentioned, to Hungerford High School. After approximately 10 years (1957) with an agreement between OCPS and Hungerford, the Northwest Orange County rural area was granted authority to construct and make operational a high school facility for persons of color within that rural sector (Apopka) to accommodate pupils from Clarcona, Lake Apopka, Plymouth, Zellwood, Fuller's Crossing, and Tangerine. Integration was yet to arrive henceforth some 12 years (1969).

In conclusion, just for a moment, all present-day

© 2015

students, of any ethnicity or area heretofore mentioned, think about the struggles and sacrifices made to ascertain a primary and secondary education by your foreparents.

These thoughts should not warrant you to be milling under stately looking oak trees, standing on street corners and storefronts, participating in illicit pharmaceutical product sales, use and abuse, robbery, and prostitution.

Having you indulging in that form of activities qualifies you having an eighth grade education granted by the "street committee" and, by the way, most pupils of this present-day dilemma cannot even properly fill out a job application. Therefore, in order to achieve in this sophisticated high technological system of innovations that society pursues daily, it is necessary to ascertain a bona fi de secondary education academic diploma.

In conjunction with an academic diploma for secondary education, you must, most definitely, insist upon yourself to steer completely away from the previous above heretofore-mentioned negative traits. Especially for Soul Brother and Soul Sister, the above events noted were extremely difficult even then within the Orange County "project" rural areas to acquire a secondary education during that era. You should undoubtedly amass constant thoughts of absolute discernment upon your gray matter in order that you don't become misled by being complacent to abnormal activities to the extent you disregard the necessity of a complete formal education. However, attendance diplomas relative to education are not the answer. Therefore, as a Bible saying goes, prepare yourself by being "fully competent" and "completely equipped." Doing so enables you to combat life's distresses.

For centuries and even more so now since the federal desegregation court order mandate still has its loopholes, numerous individuals will be misled due to many unanswered issues and problems assuming they don't need academia to survive in this system of things. Please! Believe Slim, whenever there is a "will" to achieve, numerous ways shall surely occur.

The Apopka Chief, November 25, 2011, Page 13A

Apopkan served community with zeal

Soulman for His Ghetto Community

If you believe in the tenet of creation, you believe that Jehovah God initiated life by forming humankind from dust out of the ground then blowing into man's nostrils the breath of life and thus man became a living soul. Being an entity, this soul being is regarded as being the spiritual part of a person associated with their behaviors and habits. Oh, yes!

This penning is definitely about one of God's true men, a true soul, a true Apopkan. Born in the 1890s in South Carolina, in or about the Francis Marion (Swamp Fox) National near Cordsville, S.C., where he only spent a few years of his life (approximately nine years). Due to his mother's failing health and illness requiring a warmer climate, his parents, along with a brother, assumed the trek to Jacksonville via riverboat.

Initially residing in Jacksonville, this was found not to be socially or physically beneficial to his mothers' ailments. His father decided upon recommendations from friends and family to relocate to a place called Apopka (Sarah Mead's Bottom).

Again, this entailed a laborious endeavor down the St. Johns River to Clay Springs and then to Meads Bottom. Shortly after settling at Mead's Bottom, the family attended church at Mead's Bottom and the two brothers attended the local church school that was located at the site. Eventually, most families of Negro heritage began to move below the TO&A Railroad tracks seeking homes of their own, purchasing farmland, sharecropping, employment, etc.

This particular "soul's" parents insisted that he and his brother be associated with education activities rather than farming or agricultural endeavors. This parental push, along with a favorite teacher (Olivia Pierce), influenced his appetite for achieving in education. On many occasions in years to come, he spoke to Slim about his early schooling at St. Paul AME Church in Sarah Mead's Bottom and also located at Robinson Avenue and Tenth Street east of the Consumers Lumber & Veneer Company and the Midland Railroad tracks.

This, indeed, was the beginning of his career that he so devotedly gave of himself to humankind. Upon completion of the eighth grade, he enrolled in a school of higher learning in Ohio for a period of time, then he transferred to a junior college in southeast Georgia (Georgia State Industrial College) and then later to a very prestigious Negro college (Morehouse College) in Atlanta, Ga.

Basically, he worked at hotels, cafes, riverboats, etc., during the summer months when school was out wherein to support his room, board, and tuition. When he was in his third year of college, a tragedy occurred within his family, compelling him to discontinue pursuing the academic achievement that he so desperately wanted to ascertain.

However, the advanced education that he had received up to that point in time proved to be very important within the Apopka community that he came back to serve with much zeal.

People within the exiguous area below the TO&A Railroad tracks in Apopka welcomed his trusted advice, sincerity, concerns, passion, and his honest integrity. He, too, experienced trusting his fellowman because his business survival depended upon trusting people to adhere to their obligations. He was involved in numerous debates with a Tuskegee College alumnus Arthur Willis (a tailor) who lived in Apopka, in reference to upgrading the community to better standards of living, education, and employment.

He was one of the charter members of the NAACP in Apopka along with Edwin McClary, a college alumnus. He showed in various ways support to all religious faith in Apopka below the tracks. He was also a key figure in organizing a group of Negro businesses that managed the heritage portion of Greenwood Cemetery in Apopka. This organization was responsible for the maintenance and selling of plots or grave spaces in the cemetery when he was requested to act as overseer. Over time, due to the lack of monies in the treasury of that organization, he developed a plan where the entire Negro community would go up to the cemetery on Labor Day and hold a picnic and police up the Negro portion of the cemetery.

In later years, the Negro businesses purchased a parcel of land adjacent to the east of the heritage portion of the cemetery from Dr. Thomas E. McBride, MD. After many years of struggling to maintain the cemetery, it became evident that this responsibility should be turned over to the city of Apopka. So, under his leadership, the Negro business organization turned over the remaining funds from the cemetery treasury along with the original parcel drawing (on brown meat-wrapping paper) to the city of Apopka for them to become stewards.

In 1944, he became the first scoutmaster in the ghetto of Apopka and was later on followed by Ernest Neil and James Jones Sr. As scoutmaster, he flawlessly devoted effort, time, instruction, property (for weekend camping), employment and much financial aid in order to develop the young men of the community.

James Foster, a Morehouse College alumni, was the director of Central Florida Negro Scouting, and he requested this "soulman" to set in place administrative policies and procedures for the new Negro Boy Scout

Camp in Seminole County that had so graciously been donated by W. E. Howard and named for Mr. William E. Howard and the subject of this article concurred without reservation to perform this work.

Indeed, he was still very much an advocate for education. Phyllis Wheatley High School in Apopka was in dire need in their athletic department for football equipment and a scoreboard.

He felt so compelled to assist them that he funded their need 100 percent on his own because he knew the importance of these needs to assist in furthering the education of those students involved in the sports programs. Several of these homegrown Apopka-ghetto college students and graduates will confirm that he constantly encouraged and assisted them financially in their academic efforts.

As far as his own educational aspirations, remember he had to leave college during his third year (1923-1924) because of a death in his family. Thirty-two years lapsed before he was able to accomplish his lifelong dream of receiving a bachelor of science degree from college in 1956 at Bethune-Cookman College in Daytona Beach.

92 Davis Lodge No 47 AF & AM. Michael Gladden's businesses were directly across the street from this historic building. Oldest black lodge in Florida. Photo Dr.O. 2014 12 29

This individual without any doubt left a path to follow regardless of your heritage. I must commend the Fraternal Order of Masons, Davis Lodge No 47 AF & AM of Apopka along with the city of Apopka council members (1982) in concurring to name a street in his honor. It honored the fact that he was an entrepreneur for 57 years continuously until his demise, in addition to his leadership ability in the community. It is very seldom that a person of this man's integrity comes along and you benefit by his deeds.

Take heed for the blessing Jehovah God bestowed upon us by creating an outstanding person when he made Michael Gladden Jr. He was an individual I favorably call "a soulman". He was that and he lived it each and every day within his mind and body.

Thanks from all of us.

93 The irony of a "NO DUMPING" sign in front of the Keene Road dump from West Hammon Drive. Hard earned homes now have a view of a dumpsite. Photo by DrO 2015.

Beautiful Lake Jewell is now part of landfill

Urbanization and Land Transformation

Population growth creates major changes for roadways, home construction, and light and heavy industries. Citizens, let us face reality. Whenever it pertains to deposing of waste materials, no citizen wants a waste facility placed in their area of residence. However, it is absolutely a fact that the refuse has to be disposed of in someone's backyard. Presently within the Central Florida regional area, there are six bona fide waste disposal sites.

Lake Jewell was named after Mayor John D. Jewell an elected (1926) city of Apopka mayor. The lake area was approximately 6 or 7 beautiful acres of clear water with white sand surrounding its entire body initiating at West Cleveland Street on the north side between South Central Avenue and South Washington Avenue, and West Celeste Street on its southern borders.

Near the eastern and western borders of the lake during the 1930s and 1940s were two privately owned citrus-bearing groves, each consisting of 10 acres under the management of Plymouth Citrus Growers Exchange and Winter Garden Citrus Growers. Slim recalls during the infancy years of WWII, a Boy

Scouts of America Troop 104 was donated a five-acre camping site adorned with hanging moss in the majestic oak trees. This site had 40-year-old longleaf needle pine trees and two 10-acre citrus-bearing groves in and around the Lake Jewell area. For about 30 years, prior to the designated Boy Scout camping area, Lake Jewell provided the Negro community of Apopka a public recreational area for swimming, picnics, and religious baptisms.

94 The Keene Road dump overshadows West Hammon Drive and West Celeste Street homes. Photo by DrO 2015.

This area entails a portion of the present day Class II waste disposal site. Prior to the point and time of the Class II site being placed there, the area below and beyond Lake Jewell included several surface water bodies and large citrus groves that extended to Keene

Road. More than two decades ago, this Class II facility was established and made operational in the Apopka (Orange County area) without constant scientific data monitoring and citizens' acceptance.

Whenever the subject of a waste disposal facility rears its unwanted ugly head within a proposed area that is concurred upon by our local officials with or without the masses of its citizens not being informed of its purposes and locale, it definitely arouses much apprehension within the area so designated and eventually causes havoc due to detrimental waste products producing agents that history, over a period of time, has proven, without doubt, that mankind cannot live at these contaminated sites and survive.

Currently, in the immediate area below Keene Road on McQueen Road, a proposal for a Class I facility has been brought to the attention of the residents of that entire designated area that the probability of a facility will become established and built. This proposal has aroused the concerns of citizens within a seven-mile radius as to the effects it will have on the communities of Lake Jewell, McCormick Road housing, Emerson Point, Sheeler Road housing, McCormick Road school, and below TO&A Railroad tracks to Phyllis Wheatley Elementary School. Within the past 40 years, heretofore-mentioned governmental stewardship pertaining to environmental protection of waters, lands and citizens in that immediate prescribed area have shown a lack of interest, petite or no knowledge of scientific exploration studies regarding creation of severe existing ecological problems that have become immeasurable and last but not least, inadequate funding to address issues or problems. The need for constant research is evident along with in-depth studies about the way society develops or disposes of waste products whenever they are detrimental to the ecological system including mankind.

95 Monument honoring Marvin C. Zanders at the intersection of Marvin C Zanders Avenue and Michael Gladden Boulevard. Dedicated 2010 05 31. Photo Dr. O. 2014 08 03

The Apopka Chief, December 9, 2011, Page 7B

Remembering Marvin C. Zanders Sr., the People's Choice

Odyssey of Marvin Clyde Zanders Sr. "The People's Choice"

On December 12, 2010, approximately one year ago, the demise of Marvin C. Zanders Sr. left immeasurable memories and achievements that he accomplished while being an entrepreneur and an advocate for community progress.

Although Zanders has departed from the system of things, as we know it, four of his original (1961) staff members remain. They are still performing mortuary science duties whenever requested in the likes of Billie Dean, William Albert Winchester, Alonzo Williams Jr., and William Gladden Jr. A very dear friend of mine, William Gladden Jr., indicated to me (Slim) that while attending Hungerford High School at Eatonville in the mid 1940s, even though he was several classes ahead of Mr. Marvin C. Zanders, they usually had daily conversations with each other pertaining to mortuary science that Zanders discussed with a passion in hopes he would become an outstanding funeral director and embalmer one day.

At that time, Zanders was employed part-time after school hours and weekends at Winter Park Cemetery opening and closing gravesites. This experience was very significant to the career that he chose and even more so when he acquired his own business and could not afford to hire help with the knowhow and will power to ensure his future success.

During his years at Hungerford High School in Eatonville, he would commute after classes to Orlando, to perform part-time funeral services work at Stark & Strong Funeral Home under the supervision of Willie J. Bruton, L.F.D., Emb. In later years (1960), they formed a partnership (Bruton & Zanders Funeral Home) at 31 West Michael Gladden Blvd, Apopka. During Zanders' commuting from his Winter Park home in 1948-1952 to Orlando (Starks' Funeral Home), another student, Albert McCray, ventured to Brinson Funeral Home. They would often race to see who reached their part-time funeral home job first (smile).

Willie J. Bruton and Edward Williams dismissed themselves from Stark & Strong Funeral Home and established a funeral home (B&W) in Sanford at the old Mosely Funeral Home on Sanford Avenue and encouraged Zanders to become an employee. Business for B&W was not as lucrative as anticipated and Marvin, being a newlywed, strived to accomplish his desire to become a funeral director and turned his endeavors towards mortuary science school at New York School of Embalming in the mid-1950s.

While attending school, he was employed part-time at numerous funeral homes in the New York and New Jersey areas, gaining immeasurable experiences and networking that exists even today. These professional ties have been very beneficial to each funeral establishment that he has had involvement with.

Shortly after graduating from mortuary science school, he returned to Central Florida seeking employment. However, he ventured into trade embalming and his work had him covering Central Florida and parts of west Florida. Finally, O. B. Samuels Funeral Home at Williston employed him. At this point in the latter 1950s, determination and patience were the main keys to his achieving his lifelong dream of directing funeral services.

In 1956, Glover Johnson of Eustis, and Max Stark of Orlando independently established funeral homes in Apopka. Max Stark relentlessly tried to recruit Zanders to operate a funeral home in Apopka, but Marvin declined his offer and decided to open his own establishment.

Nevertheless, there were several legal hurdles to overcome in the next few years to accomplish this lifelong goal. Although he had completed the necessary requirements at the mortuary school, the state of Florida required additional qualifications that he would obtain within one year, thus meeting Florida's laws. Zanders established his makeshift funeral home on Park Avenue and Washington Avenue in Apopka with Willie J. Bruton, L.F. D., Emb. covering for legal purposes.

At that time, all prepara tions of remains were accomplished at Bruton's Funeral Home in Orlando. Realizing he needed a proper facility, he ventured to Palmetto in 1960 to converse with a former high school friend who gladly assisted Marvin relative to extensive negotiating for a facility sought after convincing the owners of the building to grant a lease that precipitated the conception of the then-Bruton & Zanders Funeral Home to be established at 31 West Michael Gladden Blvd, Apopka.

In approximately 1969, Marvin negotiated with owners of the leased building to have lessor to enlarge to accommodate his business demands or he would purchase a building. However, the owner declined each proposal thus prompting Zanders to construct a new facility at 232 West Michael Gladden Blvd. in 1972 where it exists today.

In the early days of Bruton & Zanders Funeral Home, it served two purposes: emergency ambulance or funeral services. Fire Chief Leroy "Roy" Gilliam, City of Apopka was instrumental in training Zanders and his personnel in first aid procedures, rescue operations and driving safety for a period of 12 weeks. That enhanced training brought the personnel to a degree of quality standards that the state of Florida required.

Marvin's original staff, Albert Winchester, Trudy Grimes, Joseph "Fats" Anderson, Emmett "Poolroom Red" Underwood, Eddie Williams, Francis Pearce, Jeremiah Neil, Alonzo Williams, Fredrick Howard, Billie Dean, William Gladden Jr., and Mrs. Sarah Willis Chisholm, continued with the firm for many years into the 1980s.

However, of all the aforementioned personnel, Billie Dean, as of this penning, is the only one still affiliated with the firm.

Several persons – Wilfred A. Sanders Jr., Lloyd Sanders Sr., Greg Burrell and William Gladden Jr. – since the business was established (1961) under his supervision have attended and graduated from an accredited mortuary science school from 1969-1979 and completed the necessary state's requirements for funeral services and practices and established funeral homes in Florida, Georgia, and Pennsylvania.

History shows that several pioneer morticians prior to Zanders proprietorship in this area were Zanders mentors, including Max Stark, Richmond J. Larson, Eunice Wilson, Glover Johnson, and A.C. Brinson, all of whose professional roots initiated totally from one old firm in West Palm Beach, which was the "granddaddy" of these present-day morticians in the area.

According to Slim's observations, Slim can substantiate this entire penning due to Slim's personal association with Mr. Zanders. Slim can attest without a doubt to the readers that Marvin Zanders has achieved his ultimate goal of mortuary procedures/practices within the 20th and 21st centuries.

He personally informed Slim that he constantly encouraged his daughters, Ms. Helen J. Zanders and Ms. Beverly L. Zanders, who attended mortuary science college or college, and at some point in time, assumed duties and stewardship of the firm.

Marvin, the community thanks you for your services and contributions you have bestowed upon your fellow persons. In conclusion, "Undertaker Slim," being affiliated with "The People's Choice" since 1947, gives thanks to an outstanding individual in Marvin C. Zanders for his years of constant advice in addition to concerns and assisting his fellow man in numerous ways and means.

96 Marvin C. Zanders Funeral Home on West Michael Gladden Boulevard in Apopka, FL. Photo by DrO 2015.

97 1967 Henry Carlson, James McGraw, Glenn Woodward, Hoyt Stough, James Carter, Kenneth Eldredge.

The Pennings of Perrine Slim

The Apopka Chief, December 16, 2011, Page 9A

Many people owe Davis thanks

Favorably Called "Mr. Buddy"

Slim recalls meeting Adrene Charles Davis for the first time in 1946 when Adrene was approximately five or six years old. Most citizens nowadays refer to him as "Mr. Buddy," the dean of electricians within the tri-county area and a social security recipient at the young age of 70 years old (smile).

The meeting was orchestrated to confer with Adrene's father the elder Mr. Walter Davis Sr., a native from the state of Texas who resided in the Apopka area and was a renowned meat processor and land-clearing agent. He came to the attention of Slim's family as the results of an incident pertaining to hog-killing time that lacked Slim's family expertise regarding meat curing.

The meeting was to obtain assistance from the elder Mr. Davis on a project relative to a Boy Scout merit badge program Slim had undertaken pertaining to the study and raising of hogs during the WWII era. At the time and because of his age, "Mr. Buddy" had no interest in domestic hog breeding. Even nowadays, "Mr. Buddy" and Slim often refer to the old wooden smokehouse that's still intact on the Davis estate where his father cured Slim's meats in the 1940s.

Adrene's brother, James Davis, a professor,

politician, lobbyist, and entrepreneur was indeed the prime catalyst and teacher for the development of Adrene's vocational skills relative to electric installation and repairs. While "Mr. Buddy" was enrolled (1954-57) at Jones High School in Orlando, he was enticed to pursue the study of electrical installation practices and procedures in addition to performing hands-on work experience after classes on a daily basis. In the early 1960s, the Davis Brothers established an electric installation and repair service that existed for more than 45 years.

Mr. Buddy, Adrene Charles Davis, there are many people who owe you thanks for the work you have completed to help them see the light.

The Apopka Chief, December 23, 2011, Page 16A

Vernon McQueen was prominent alumnus of Wheatley High School

Phyllis Wheatley High School Sports Hall of Fame

Prior to Thanksgiving, Slim had the privilege to talk with Vernon McQueen, one of the prominent alumni of Phyllis Wheatley High School of Apopka. Mr. McQueen was an excellent student and an outstanding athlete while enrolled in addition to graduating from PWHS at Apopka in the sixth decade of the 1900s. Mr. McQueen, upon completing the required academic requirements for secondary education, continued his academic skills and athleticism at South Carolina State College in Orangeburg, S.C., during the course of a four-year stay wherein he earned a bachelor of science degree. Since graduating, he has ventured into several arenas of gainful employments that required bachelor's degrees namely state of New York (juvenile delinquency division), New York City Department of Education, and Progress Energy of Florida (energy conservation).

During the course of our lengthy conversations relative to student athletes, it was suggested that Perrine Slim pen briefl y about those "dinosaurs" athletes of PWHS origin (smile).

In and around the late 1940s, Apopka Junior High

School at 18th Street initiated its basketball affiliations within the school district. The first basketball coaches consisted of Ms. Argrett and Ms. Woodard who, through their dedication, concerns, and expertise, would eventually build the team into a powerhouse of roundball in the district. At that point, the school was named Apopka Junior High School, and was later changed to honor the Negro poetess, Phillis Wheatley. In 2009 in the *The Apopka Chief*, there was a Bits 'n' Tips column penning by Perrine Slim relative to student-athletes of a designated era who lived in Northwest Orange County and attended Apopka Junior High School and Phyllis Wheatley Elementary until 1957. Nevertheless, Phyllis Wheatley High School (PWHS) at that point in time was non-existent in the immediate Apopka area as a high school. Approximately 1951, the ninth-grade curriculum was initiated at the Apopka Junior High School that in later years came to be known as Phyllis Wheatley High School, in addition to construction of a modern gymnasium. Ms. Jones became the first coach to coach in the gym and in 1952, the famous illustrious basketball, football, track and field, and dancing coach Booker T. Reddick was added to the staff.

This transformation from a clay basketball facility in the heretofore-mentioned era precipitated the trek of Apopka Junior High School on its way to be known locally, statewide and nationally as a powerhouse in the world of sports.

Pioneer and trailblazer players, the likes of Louis "Nick" Garvin, Lee "Mickey" Neal Jr., Joseph "Shoe" Gladden, Richard "Beck" Washington, Herman "Doc" McQueen, Johnnie "Bubba" Stokes, Willie James "Dog" Fillmore, James "Syrup" Davis, Malachi "Cow" Woods, Clinton "Form" Moss, Quilley Freeman, Robert Lee "Hip" Brown, Frank "Hog" Baker, Leroy "Booney" Fillmore, George Marshall, and Huff Henry. Several student athletes of the era (1951-1959) who participated religiously in sports programs later on became accomplished athletes in football and basketball at several historically black colleges and universities as well as semi-pro basketball and major league baseball.

It's Slim's intention in this penning to emphasize the selection of inductees (student athletes) from the period of time covering 1957-1968 by the 2011 Mass Reunion Committee.

The students identified that were ascertained to have academically qualified and graduated while enrolled at Phyllis Wheatley High School in Apopka are:

1957 - Cleo Sanders

1958 – Ethel Jean Cooks and Herbert Graham

1959 – Mary Pollard and Willie "Goose" Thomas

1960 – Geraldine Bridges and Freddie Fillmore

1961 – Betty Everett and the late Ernest "Big Pop" James

1962 – Marion White and Robert Board

1963 – Martha Everett and Larry Rozier

1964 – Elizabeth Robinson and Manuel Thomas

1965 – Annie Pearl Swift and Vernon McQueen

1966 – Carolyn Richardson and the late Calvin White

1967 – Barbara Wynn and Dover Wynn

1968 – Charles Richardson

It is with great appreciation and thanks to the 2011 Reunion Committee that the accomplishments of these individuals has been noted.

The Pennings of Perrine Slim

Majority of Negroes disregard political experience, creed

Political Concerns of Citizens in the Ghetto

Although the presidential election for November 2012 is less than 12 months away, it has been an uplifting episode for citizens who are of voting age and will vote in the upcoming election. This has been precipitated and orchestrated through the Republican Party debates that many voters use to evaluate those Republican candidates pertaining to their platforms and issues as they strive to run for president of these great United States.

This Receipt is furnished under Section 11, Chapter 5596, Laws of Florida. ERNEST AMOS, Comptroller.
August, 1919.

CAPITATION OR POLL TAX FOR 1919—STATE OF FLORIDA, ORANGE COUNTY.

No. 627

Orlando, Fla., _____, 19____

Received of _____ the sum of ONE DOLLAR in payment of his Capitation or Poll Tax for the Year A. D. Nineteen Hundred and Nineteen (1919).

Color ____ Age ____ No. Election District 6

T. J. Appleyard, Printer, Tallahassee, Fla.   Tax Collector, Orange County.

98 M. Gladden poll tax for 1919 paid in 1920 for the hard fought right for black men to vote. Photo of original doc DrO 2015

The debates have been extremely beneficial for persons regardless of profession or ethnicity as they pursue a better understanding of election procedures/ practices, platform study and unresolved issues regarding potential candidates.

Whether you have a designated party affiliation or are nonpartisan relative to these Republican Party debates for the 2012 presidential election, debates haven't created this much curiosity since Ronald Reagan ran for president.

Slim recalls the national presidential and Orange County Sheriff elections in 2008 that separated individuals from their party affiliations precipitated by age, ethnicity, creed, or county section.

Kelsey McFarley, Ph.D.., and community social scientist who was nurtured in the Zellwood- Apopka area, participated in a Florida State program relative to politics since the 2008 election. McFarley and Slim have corresponded continuously over the years, gathering information and addressing concrete facts and issues in reference to statutes pertaining to election procedures and practices.

It was in 2008, that Slim last met within one of the Apopka areas (ghetto, Soulsville, project, hood, blackbelt, and bottom) with Dr. McFarley and his Democratic constituents in the likes of Ms. Linda Baldwin, Jeremy Robinson, Antonio Edmond, James West, Lionel Griffin, Tony Robinson, Ms. Amanda Swift, V. "Haitian Jean" St. Jean, and several others not intentionally omitted. However, numerous issues relative to this meeting have pyramided to the point of creating negative resolutions by the Democratic majority.

These resolutions are not plausible to the point where the masses of citizens will understand and abide them. Slim will admit that his party affiliation has been Republican since he was of voting age in and around the fifth decade of the 1900s.

In conclusion, it is Slim's opinion that during those brief conferences in 2008, and even nowadays, too much emphasis was placed on several factors, including the dislike for the Republican Party by the majority of Negroes, a disregard for lack of political experience, ethnicity and creed.

Perrine Slim

Perrine Slim, Apopka nutured, attended his first eight years of formal education at the Clarcona Colored School. He then attended Hungerford High School, a private school for people of color, in completion of his twelve years of education.

Slim is a Korean War veteran of the U.S. Navy on the USS General Mann TAP

112. He proudly served from 1951-1954, Korean War era, above the 38th Parallel.

99 William Gladden, Jr. serving on the USS General Mann TAP 112 above the 38th Parallel, Korean War. From W. Gladden.

Work took Perrine Slim from Apopka, to New York, to Miami. His heart has always been in citrus production.

100 **William Gladden, Jr. at sea in front of a gun turret.**
Photo from William Gladden.

Index

Olmstead Publishing LLC

© 2015

Olmstead Publishing LLC

43027016R10267

Made in the USA
Charleston, SC
15 June 2015